# CULTURE AND EMOTIONAL ECONOMY OF MIGRATION

This book studies how the act of migration is a motivating constituent in the production of popular culture in both the homeland and the destination. It looks at the formations of cultures in the process of identity-making of approximately 200 million Indians scattered across the world, from colonial to contemporary times. The volume is an in-depth exploration of the flow of cultures and their interactions through a study of North Indian migrants who underwent two waves of emigration – from the Bhojpuri region to the Dutch colony of Suriname between 1873 and 1916 to work on sugar, coffee, cotton and cocoa plantations, and their descendants who moved to the Netherlands following the Surinamese independence in 1975. It compares this complex network of cultures among the migrants to the folk culture of the Bhojpuri region from where large-scale migration is still taking place.

Drawing on archival records, secondary literature, folk songs, rare photographs and extensive fieldwork across continents – the Bhojpuri region, Mumbai, Surat and Ghaziabad in India and Suriname and the Netherlands – this book will be useful to scholars and researchers of culture studies, labour studies, sociology, modern Indian history, migration and diaspora studies. It will also interest the Indian diaspora, especially in Europe and the Americas.

**Badri Narayan** is Professor at the Centre for the Study of Discrimination and Exclusion, School of Social Sciences, Jawaharlal Nehru University, New Delhi, India. He previously taught at the G.B. Pant Social Science Institute, Allahabad. His research interests range from popular culture, social and anthropological history to Dalit and subaltern issues. Writing in English and Hindi, Narayan is the author of *Kanshiram: Leader of the Dalits* (2014), *The Making of the Dalit Public in North India: Uttar Pradesh, 1950–Present* (2011), *Fascinating Hindutva: Saffron Politics and Dalit Mobilisation* (2009), and *Women Heroes and Dalit Assertion in North India* (2006). He has been the recipient of the Fulbright Senior Fellowship (2004–2005) and the Smuts Fellowship, University of Cambridge (2007).

# CULTURE AND EMOTIONAL ECONOMY OF MIGRATION

*Badri Narayan*

LONDON AND NEW YORK

First published 2017
by Routledge

2 Park Square, Milton Park, Abingdon, Oxfordshire OX14 4RN
52 Vanderbilt Avenue, New York, NY 10017

*Routledge is an imprint of the Taylor & Francis Group, an informa business*

First issued in paperback 2019

Copyright © 2017 Badri Narayan

The right of Badri Narayan to be identified as author of this work has been asserted by him in accordance with sections 77 and 78 of the Copyright, Designs and Patents Act 1988.

All rights reserved. No part of this book may be reprinted or reproduced or utilised in any form or by any electronic, mechanical, or other means, now known or hereafter invented, including photocopying and recording, or in any information storage or retrieval system, without permission in writing from the publishers.

Notice:
Product or corporate names may be trademarks or registered trademarks, and are used only for identification and explanation without intent to infringe.

*British Library Cataloguing in Publication Data*
A catalogue record for this book is available from the British Library

*Library of Congress Cataloging-in-Publication Data*
A catalog record has been requested for this book.

ISBN: 978-1-138-20179-8 (hbk)
ISBN: 978-0-367-17734-8 (pbk)

Typeset in Bembo
by Apex CoVantage, LLC

Dedicated to

my friends Susan and Maurits

This book is based on two projects: 'BIDESIA – Exhibition and Research on the Dynamics of Migration, Social Development and Cultural Identity' and 'Migration and Cultural Traditions of Bhojpuri Region'. It has drawn from the significant research and academic contribution of Maurits Hassankhan, Narinder Mohkamsingh, Elizabeth den Boer, and Sahiensha Ramdas (Suriname), Susan Legene and Chitra Gajadin (the Netherlands), and Mousumi Majumder and Nivedita Singh (India).

Chapter 2 (*Bidesia* and settlement histories in Suriname) evolved from sections of the Suriname report of the Bidesia project (by Maurits Hassankhan and team) published in the resource book *Kahe Gaile Bides* (Allahabad: Mango Books, 2010).

Chapter 3 (Double migration and silenced history) evolved from sections of the Netherlands report of the Bidesia project (by Susan Legene and Chitra Gajadin) published in the resource book *Kahe Gaile Bides* (Allahabad: Mango Books, 2010).

Chapter 4 (*Bidesia* folk culture in the triangle) evolved from a combination of India and the Netherlands reports and a section of the Surinamese reports (by Narinder Mohkamsingh and Sahiensha Ramdas) of the Bidesia project published in the resource book *Kahe Gaile Bides* (Allahabad: Mango Books, 2010).

*Kai Kehli Chukwa Ki Choral Mulukwa Tu?*
*Kehal Na Dilwa Ke Halia Balmua*
(What crime have I committed that you left the country and did not tell me your feelings before leaving?)
    – Bhikhari Thakur, *Bidesia* (Yadav and Sinha 2005: 37)

# CONTENTS

|   |   |   |
|---|---|---|
| *List of figures* | | x |
| *Preface* | | xii |
| *Acknowledgements* | | xiv |
| | Introduction | 1 |
| 1 | Who migrated and why: the *bidesia* story | 26 |
| 2 | *Bidesia* and settlement histories in Suriname (*With Maurits Hassankhan*) | 38 |
| 3 | Double migration and silenced history: Hindustanis from Suriname to the Netherlands | 59 |
| 4 | *Bidesia* folk culture in the triangle: Bhojpuri region of India, Suriname and the Netherlands (*With Narinder Mohkamsingh*) | 64 |
| 5 | Still they are migrating: contemporary migration from Bhojpuri region | 107 |
| 6 | Migration and cultural productions: documenting history of cultural practices | 133 |
| 7 | Migration and politics | 153 |
| | Conclusion | 159 |
| | *Bibliography* | 164 |
| | *Index* | 169 |

# FIGURES

1.1 Travelling Coolies. Photograph: Ds P.M. Legene 1914.
Collection Tropenmuseum 60048465   30
2.1 Recruiting Areas for Suriname. Based on
De Klerk (1953: 47)   41
2.2 Group Portrait of Hindustani Indentured Labourers.
Photograph: Julius Muller before 1895. Collection
Surinaams Museum   42
2.3 Hindustanis in Suriname, Wearing Traditional Costumes
during Festivities in Front of the Government Palace at
the Main Square in Paramaribo. Photograph: Augusta
Curiel c. 1923. Collection Tropenmuseum 60006535   43
2.4 Hindustanis in Suriname with a *Tajiya*, c. 1890.
Photograph: Julius Muller, before 1895. Collection
Tropenmuseum 60005593   46
2.5 Hindustanis Wearing Ram Lila Costumes at a
Performance on a Location between Paramaribo and
Uitkijk, in Suriname. Photograph: C. van der Koppel c.
1930–1940. Collection Tropenmuseum 10019302   50
2.6 Portrait of a Hindustani Woman in Suriname.
Photographer Unknown, between 1900 and 1920.
Collection Tropenmuseum 10019396 and 60006494   51
2.7 Sarees and Bangles in a Hindustani Supermarket in
Rotterdam. Photograph: Sarojini Lewis, 2006   55
3.1 Group Portrait of Women and Children, Hindustani
Indentured Labourers. Photograph: Julius Muller before
1895. Collection Tropenmuseum 60008925   60
3.2 Hindu Gods in the House of a Hindustani Migrant
from Suriname in the Netherlands. Photograph: Sarojini
Lewis, 2006   61

# FIGURES

4.1 Hindustani Musicians during a Wedding Party in Suriname, Posing with Their Instruments Sarangi, *Dantal* and Dhol. Photograph: J. Dzn. Blaauboer 1952. Collection Tropenmuseum 10020893 — 83

5.1 Migrants Outside a Station Waiting for Their Trains to Go to Their Destination. Photograph: Brijendra Gautam, December 2014 — 112

5.2 Women in Barwaripur Village, Sultanpur District, Uttar Pradesh, Sharing Their Folk Forms. Photograph: Brijendra Gautam, December 2014 — 116

6.1 *Birha* Folk Singer Mannu Yadav Giving His Performance during a Cultural Meet. Photograph: Brijendra Gautam, January 2016 — 135

6.2 Folk Singer Mannu Yadav Performing *Birha* Using *Kartal*. Photograph: Brijendra Gautam, January 2016 — 137

6.3 *Sankata Mata* Temple in Varanasi Where Women Go to Offer Prayers for the Well-Being of Their Migrant Husbands — 148

7.1 Village Women Happily Narrating Their Folk Cultural Forms, in Baderi Village, Jaunpur District, Uttar Pradesh, India. Photograph: Brijendra Gautam, November 2015 — 154

7.2 Bhojpuri Singer Dinesh Lal Yadav 'Nirhauwa' Giving His Performance at the Time of Elections in Mumbai. Photograph: Brijendra Gautam, October 2014 — 157

# PREFACE

This book explores the making of the culture of migration from the past to the present. The major happening that played a crucial role in the formation of the culture of migration was indentured migration (1873–1916) from the Bhojpuri region of India. Today also the phenomenon of migration is visible in those villages from where indentured migration took place in the past. The *longue dureé* of the culture of migration consists of indentured past and contemporary migration to cities like Mumbai, Ahmedabad, Surat, Gaziabad and other big cities. This book explores the *bidesia bhav* and emotional history of migration in the homeland and destination while looking at the formation and function of the culture of migration.

In the pre-colonial period when the European world was extending its domain across the globe through its colonies, it needed a huge source of cheap and abundant labour to work in the sugar, coffee, jute and other plantations in these colonies. After the abolition of slavery, it found this source of labour in the Bhojpuri region of India. Between the mid-nineteenth century and the early twentieth century, a large number of indentured labourers were sent from this region to various European colonies like Suriname, Mauritius, Fiji, Guyana and Trinidad, under an agreement signed between the British government and the governments of other colonial countries like Holland and France. Although many labourers returned to India after the expiry of their contract, a sizeable number remained behind even after these countries were decolonized, and their descendants now form a significant minority group there. This can be evidenced from the fact that in Suriname the Hindustani population numbers some 150,000 today while the population of Hindustanis who migrated to Holland when the Surinamese attained independence in 1975 is around 100,000.

The Surinamese Hindustanis and the Dutch Hindustanis have now imbibed the culture and heritage of their destination countries, but they have also preserved the language and culture of their ancestors who migrated from India long ago. This culture is the common heritage of the Surinamese Hindustanis, the Dutch Hindustanis and the Bhojpuris of India. That this common culture has withstood the test of time can be evidenced from the fact that even after so many generations one can observe a striking similarity in the oral culture of these three sets of people.

# ACKNOWLEDGEMENTS

This book is an offshoot of two research projects, that is 'BIDESIA – Exhibition and Research on the Dynamics of Migration, Social Development and Cultural Identity in the Bhojpuri Region of India, in Suriname and the Netherlands' and 'Migration and Cultural Traditions of Bhojpuri Region: A Research and Documentation Programme' sponsored by the Tata Trusts, Mumbai. BIDESIA was an international exhibition and cultural exchange project launched in 2005 involving three institutes and museums in the three countries concerned, namely India, Suriname and the Netherlands, and was designed with the aim of documenting the common cultural heritage of these three sets of people sharing a common descent. The project resulted in the publication of three country reports. The Bidesia Resource Book *Kahe Gaile Bides: Why Did You Go Overseas?* was published in 2010 by Mango Press, Allahabad, India. The contents of the resource book were compiled and edited by Mousumi Majumder. The editorial board comprised Badri Narayan Tiwari (India), Maurits Hassankhan (Suriname) and Susan Legene (the Netherlands) with contributions by Badri Narayan Tiwari and Nivedita Singh (India), Narinder Mohkamsingh, Elizabeth den Boer, Sahiensha Ramdas and Maurits Hassankhan (Suriname) and Chitra Gajadin (The Netherlands). The Netherlands Country report entitled 'A Silenced History: Hindustani Migration to Suriname and Holland' prepared by Chitra Gajadin was printed in October 2005 by KIT. The Surinamese report was prepared by Maurits Hassankhan and was printed in 2008. The project 'Migration and Cultural Traditions of Bhojpuri Region' was launched in 2013 as a humble endeavour to trace, preserve and provide an acknowledged platform to several unsung rural poets, folk story tellers, singers and performers who stood strongly against the winds of change. The materials and the empirical data base generated during the second ongoing project provide a rich relevant research base for the book.

# ACKNOWLEDGEMENTS

I would like to express my heartfelt gratitude to the KIT Tropenmuseum–Royal Tropical Institute (TM), Amsterdam, and IMWO, Paramaribo, Suriname, and G.B. Pant Social Science Institute, Allahabad, for ensuring the smooth sailing of the project. Their trust and confidence in me are the shining lights that have constantly guided me in my endeavours. I would like to thank Chitra Gajadin for providing us an excellent report on 'Double Migration and Silenced Histories of Surinamese Hindustanis in the Netherlands.' I would like to make a special mention of Dr Narinder Mohkamsingh for his valuable contribution to the chapter *bidesia* folk culture in the triangle: Bhojpuri region of India, Suriname and the Netherlands with a special focus on Hindustani music and drama in Suriname. I would like to express my special thanks to Sahiensha Ramdas who provided a note on the life and work of Goeroepersad Nirandjan, a drama writer, poet, director and so on. Thanks are also due to Ms Chitra Gajadin, Sahiensha Ramdas and Elizabeth den Boer who provided the able assistantship in Holland and Suriname. I would also like to thank Maurits Hassankhan and Susan Legene for their valuable contributions to the book. In addition we would like to thank HGIS-cultuurfonds (Dutch Ministry of Foreign Affairs and Dutch Ministry of Education, Culture and Science), Mondriaan Stichting/Erfgoed Minderheden Project and Prins Claus Fonds, the Netherlands (cultural initiatives in non-Western societies), who understood the relevance of this project and agreed to fund it. We would also like to thank the Tata Trusts, Mumbai, for sponsoring the project 'Migration and Cultural Traditions of Bhojpuri Region – A Research and Documentation Programme'. Thanks are due to Archana Singh, assistant professor, GBPI and co-director of the project, team members of the project Mousumi Majumder, Ritu Sureka, Brijendra Gautam, Tinku Paul, Nivedita Singh, Julie Khanna, Jai Prakash Tripathi, Vandana Mishra, Kulendra Nath and Shobhnath and all the other staff members of Dalit Resource Center, GBPI, for their support and cooperation. Finally, heartfelt thanks are due to the director of GBPI, Prof. Pradeep Bhargava, for all his help and support.

Last but not least we would like to thank all the respondents who graciously narrated to us their stories and shared with us their cultural heritage. Without their enthusiastic participation the project could not have been accomplished.

# INTRODUCTION

In the colonial period when the European colonial countries like the United Kingdom, France and the Netherlands were extending their domain across the globe through their colonies, they set up a large number of sugar, coffee, cocoa, jute and other plantations in some of the Caribbean countries that were their colonies like Suriname, Fiji, Mauritius, Guyana and Trinidad. These plantations, which were owned and overseen by Europeans from the colonial countries, needed labourers to work in them. After the abolition of slavery from the world, the Bhojpuri region was viewed by the British colonial government as a potential source of cheap labour (Majumder 2010: 11). Emigration from the Bhojpuri region started in 1834 to Mauritius, in 1838 to Guiana and in 1845 to the other British Caribbean colonies. The push factor was the presence of a huge surplus labour there. People were more willing to migrate from the Bhojpuri region to these colonies in the aftermath of the 1857 revolution that had drained the region of all its resources, leaving the maximum population in poverty and misery. The frequent famines and droughts affecting the region also brought abject scarcity and destitution in their wake and left the entire region reeling under acute unemployment and penury. Thus under an agreement between the British government and the governments of the Netherlands and France, the period between the late nineteenth century and the early twentieth century saw huge populations of Indians, who were mostly Bhojpuris but also included people from the Braj, Awadh and Magahi regions of Bihar and Uttar Pradesh, being sent to work in their overseas plantations as indentured labourers for a period of five years (ibid).

The departure of these migrants caused untold grief, both to the persons who were left behind and to the persons who were leaving the country for foreign shores. The expression of this grief at this separation gave birth to a distinct folk culture in the Bhojpuri region. Since *bidesia* (from the word *bidesh* meaning 'foreign') was the term used to refer to migrant labourers by the people who were left behind, '*bidesia* folk culture' is the name given to this folk cultural tradition. This cultural tradition is represented in many forms like *nautanki* (musical theatre), dramas, folk songs and folk paintings. It is a holistic folklore tradition, which revolves around the theme of the departure of the migrant Bhojpuris. Thus the term *bidesia* is in one sense used as an affectionate term for non-resident Bhojpuris and in another sense refers to the folk tradition that was created in memory of these non-resident Bhojpuris (ibid: 11–12). 'Folklore' refers to the documentation of the long-term collective memory of the migrants that is expressed in metaphors, symbols, tone and tunes of the migrants. One of the important constituents of the collective memory of the migrant is emotion, which is expressed through pain and compassion. The folk songs contain the element of pain and compassion and preserve the changes that have been happening in the society since long. Emotions are the base of social memory of the migrant and are also visible in their language. The words used in their language that reflect migration are the result of their pain of separation and the feeling of compassion within them. These words have their own tone and long tunes and explicitly express the migrant's pain of separation.

It is interesting to note that parallel to the *bidesia* folk culture that was emerging and developing in India, similar folk cultures were also developing in the countries that were the destinations of the Bhojpuri Indians. This was because when the *bidesias* left their native lands for unknown destinations, they took with them their cultural baggage that consisted of both intangible and tangible artefacts like their folk songs, folk tales, oral memories of their native places and also copies of *Ramayana, Hanuman Chalisa*, Qur'an and hadith, folk stories, Kabir poems, sacred thread and other items of daily use like a Queen Victoria rupee, in order to keep alive the memories of their native lands (Majumder 2010: 12). These cultural artefacts were diligently passed down over the generations to their descendants who remained behind in these countries even after the period of contract ended and the countries were decolonized. Although at present these people of Indian origin have become a part of the native population of these countries and form significant minority groups there, they have preserved the language and culture of their ancestors who migrated from the Bhojpuri region long ago as their cultural heritage; however, they have also imbibed the culture and language of their destination countries through a long process of acculturation. The study of their present language and culture throws light on the process of continuity and change undergone by the Hindustanis over the years and also contributes to the strengthening of cultural bonds between the Bhojpuris living in India and the large population of Bhojpuri diaspora spread out across the globe (Majumder 2010: 12).

One of the countries that were the destinations for the Bhojpuris who were sent to work as labourers on the sugarcane, coffee, cotton and cocoa plantations was Suriname, which was under the control of the Dutch. Between 26 February 1873 and 24 May 1916, about 34,000 Hindustanis from the Bhojpuri region migrated to Suriname. Some generations later, around the year of Surinamese independence in 1975, a large number of Surinamese Hindustanis migrated to the Netherlands. These Dutchmen of Hindustani descent constitute a significant minority group within the Dutch society. In Suriname too, the Hindustanis form a large percentage of the total population of the country. The historical background in international migration, from India to Suriname, and from Suriname to the Netherlands, provides the basis for a common cultural heritage of people in three regions in the world since the cultural baggage that had been taken to Suriname and passed down to their descendants by the first-generation Bhojpuri migrants was also carried by the Surinamese Hindustanis when they migrated to Holland. In this process, the practices, customs and rituals that had begun to be eroded in their native countries were preserved among both the Surinamese Hindustanis and the Dutch Hindustanis. Myths about the past started coming into being as well, and multiple cultural practices changed, with many of the original meanings being either added to or forgotten (ibid: 12–13).

However, in spite of the changes that have taken place in all the three countries over the years, there is a striking similarity in the culture of these three sets of people, which shows that many aspects of the common heritage shared by these three sets of Indians, that is the Surinamese Hindustanis, the Dutch Hindustanis and the Bhojpuri Indians, have withstood the test of time. In each of these regions, migration histories are anchored in places, in material objects, in cultural practices and in common knowledge that form an important aspect of a collective identity. Places that remind one of migration stories are, for instance, village wells, ponds, rivers, quays, fortresses, shipwrecks, peculiar trees and sugar mills both in India and in Suriname; 'tangible objects' may be personal belongings, photographs, archives and art. Migration memory is also 'intangible', travelling around the world in the words, the minds and the knowledge of people, as well as staying behind in the memory, songs and plays of those who saw others leave. Thus the dynamics of migration, social development and cultural identity make it clear that roots are not just 'bonds' fixed in the past; roots themselves are dynamic as well; they also have a history, which can be seen both in the intangible form in the art and literature and in the tangible form in the cultural artefacts of all three countries. Linking together these aspects of migrant culture in the three regions concerned will deepen our understanding and appreciation of the role of culture in migrant community development and acculturation processes (ibid).

Here I would also like to discuss the notion of hybridity as proposed by Homi K. Bhabha, who is considered by some as the father of hybrid theory. Hybridity applies contextually to the flow of cultures and their interactions. Bhabha argued that colonizers and the colonized are mutually dependent in constructing a shared culture. According to him, hybridity is a key feature of post-colonial identity. He argues that the nature of colonial identity is not monolithic but ambiguous or hybrid and the interaction is even asymmetrical between the culture of the colonizer and the colonized.[1] Applied to migration processes, hybridity denotes the simultaneous action of subjects in diverse cultural systems, resulting in the creation of new cultural articulations and socialities and 'hybrid cultural identities'. For instance, the *Sarnami* language of Suriname is a mix of various dialects of India. Even though *Sarnami* is a mix of various dialects, its base dialect is Bhojpuri because it constitutes the verb and we can determine the nature of language from the verb and not from the noun and pronoun. In the destination there are new developments in the folk songs, folk forms and food habits of the migrants. In spite of all these new developments, the base culture of the community is retained. The migrants' festive occasions are incomplete without their base food habits like *dhal puri*, which they have brought in from Indian Bhojpuri culture. If we understand the base of the cultural composition of a community, we find that even in the domain of hybridity the base culture of a community is retained like the Bhojpuris in Suriname have tried to preserve their original culture. On the basis of the base food, base dialect and base cultural behaviour, other elements get associated with the culture, giving rise to a hybrid and mixed culture. Even in the migration taking place internally, we get to see the effect of destination in the homeland.

Baderi village is situated twenty-eight kilometers west of Jaunpur district in Uttar Pradesh. It falls under the block Sheetalraj. Baderi is a Brahmin-dominated village with only one Kumhar household. Mostly the youth of this village have migrated to metropolitan cities like Mumbai for a livelihood. The migrants increase their income in the destination by playing orchestra, dholak and other musical instruments and also by singing songs. On the occasion of festivals, the village people organize cultural programmes, which are attended by a large number of youth and elderly people in the village. A big fair is organized here on the occasion of *Vijayadashmi*, which attracts people from districts like Allahabad, Bhadohi, Pratapgarh and also other adjacent villages. I observed in the fair that the men and womenfolk of the village were purchasing items for their use like the farmers were busy buying the tools like *khurpi* (trowel), *hansia* (sickle) and *fawda* (spade) that would help them in their fields. The women were busy buying items of their everyday use as well as items to adorn themselves. Not only traditional food items like *jalebi, kachalu, chaat, gatta lai, sohan halwa* and *khaja* allured the people, but we also saw the crowd gathering at the fast food stalls like pav bhaji, chow mein and burger. The effect of destination was clearly visible in the homeland. The people of Baderi village who migrate to cities within India like Mumbai, Ahmedabad and Surat for a better livelihood are introducing the cultural heritage of their destination points in their homeland. *Garbha* is a popular folk dance form of Gujarat. The migrants who return from Gujarat have introduced this folk dance form in their homeland. We saw the village people performing *garbha* on the occasion of Dussehra. Thus we see that a common cultural heritage is paving its way in the homeland, but this is not hybridity. Various elements get associated with each other due to their interactive processes, and hybridity is formed in this manner. The problem of the notion of hybridity is that it does not recognize the base element in the cultural composition of a community.[2]

## Migration and making of emotional community

The diasporic community always idealizes the homeland because it is physically absent from the homeland and consequently in most cases remains socially excluded from the host society. This idea gives rise to the often occurring problem of finding a place where diaspora belong and they are trapped in between the homeland and the host country even though globalization has made it easier to access their homelands. However, they reap the benefits of their destination countries, which allow for upward social or class mobility, but even within these beneficial economic circumstances diasporic subjects describe themselves as feeling trapped. They often claim to live in the hyphen of the two countries since the hyphen acts as something that separates as well as joins two terms. Although this space offers opportunities, it is also a hybrid space and leads to identity crises among the diaspora. On the other hand, diaspora no longer necessarily creates a condition that involves trauma and marginalization but also leads to empowerment and enrichment. This happens because of the crossing of nation-state boundaries, which allows the diaspora to view themselves not as minorities but as transnational subjects. Dipesh Chakrabarty, while talking about the notion of home in Bengal around 1950s, has distinctly placed the difference between a temporary place of residence and one's ancestral dwelling by use of two different words *bhasha* (dialect) and *baari* (home). While the former depicts the transient residence, the latter associates the ancestral home (Chakrabarty 2002: 120).

In the context of the mass migration from the Bhojpuri region to various destinations across the globe during the colonial period, which was often forced in nature, the situation was very different since migrants had to survive in adverse conditions while coping with the grief of separation from loved ones. Many migrants became victims of anxiety and trauma, as is evident from autobiographies and letters. This sorrow was also pervasive in the homeland where family members of migrants had to cope with the trauma of the virtual 'disappearance' of loved ones. Official colonial narratives based on the conclusions of the Sanderson Commission of 1912, which was appointed by the Colonial Office to consider ways of improving the system, however claimed that the migration was in the economic interests of Indian labourers who were providing 'the greatest assistance' in increasing the prosperity of recipient colonies and that the indenture was the only practical form of emigration to distant colonies on any considerable scale.[3] These commissions highlighted such things as the opportunities available to Indians in the colonies to acquire land and called for the system to be judged purely on its economic results, ignoring a host of social and psychological problems attendant on such migration.

Even historians writing about indentured migration rarely speak of the emotions of migrants and their family members who were separated from them since the historiography consisted mainly of official records created by the government or the colonial elite, including Christian churches and missionaries. It was only after scholars from the Indian diaspora began pursuing their own research agenda that a historiographical change occurred, with an attempt to reinterpret this history from the point of view of the labourers themselves (Hassankhan 2013). Fijian scholar Brij V. Lal, who pioneered the use of statistical material, has argued that while statistical analysis provided valuable details about trends and tendencies, it did not provide insight into the motives and perceptions of the emigrants themselves. He advocated the use of Hindi folk songs, 'which can movingly illuminate the feelings of the emigrants about various aspects of indenture' (Lal 1980: 66). Peter and Carol Stearns also suggest the importance of oral and folk sources to understand emotional issues related to social processes.[4]

The role of emotions in indentured migration is crucial since this ongoing movement of large numbers of people over many decades broke various familial and village ties in almost every household. The places to which migrants were taken were long distances away, which made visiting loved ones almost impossible. The most practical means of communication, letter writing, took almost six months to reach their destinations. In the homelands the separation was probably more traumatic since those left behind probably had little idea where their loved ones had gone, how far away it was and the exact nature of work, especially in the early period. This was disclosed by the Sanderson Commission, which concluded that only 25 per cent of people knew where they were going.[5] Autobiographies of indentured migrants suggest that they were lured to the colonies under false promises and were also not told how far the place was.[6] The observation of prominent nationalist leader G.K. Gokhale supports the views of the indentured autobiographers such as Munsi Rahman Khan when he called for a prohibition of recruitment of Indian labour in the Imperial Legislative Council on 4 March 1912 on the grounds that the system was 'based on fraud and maintained by force ... a system so wholly opposed to modern sentiments of justice and humanity is a grave blot on the civilisation of any country that tolerates it' (Mangru 1993).

Migration is usually looked upon as an economic phenomenon, but it has strong social, cultural and political effects in both the homeland and the destination. The most important consequence of migration is that it unleashes a flood of emotions among various sets of people separated from each other, which is invisible and thus difficult to quantify. Several studies have been made on the lives of indentured migrants in various Caribbean countries like Guyana, Fiji, Trinidad, Mauritius and Suriname. While most of them are literary and include autobiographies, poetry and stories based on the diaspora, many are also scholarly and academic writings on the social, economic and political aspects of indentured migration from India. Some of them are Tinker (1993), Vatuk (1964), Singh (1998), Carter (2002), Hill (1919), McNeill and Lal (1915), Brereton and Dookeran (1982), Richmond (2010), Khan (2005), Totaram (1991), Erickson (1934), Naidu (1980) and Walter (1981).

There is also a need to mention about some of the well-researched and well-written scholarly works on the Indian diaspora, including the recent *Indians in Kenya: The Politics of Diaspora* (Cambridge: Harvard University Press, 2015) by Sana Aiyar; *Women, Labour & Politics in Trinidad & Tobago: A History*, the classic works by Rhoda Reddock and *East Indians in Trinidad: A Study in Cultural Persistence* by Morton Klass, not to mention the eminent scholar Ravindra K. Jain's comprehensive *Indian Transmigrants: Malaysian and Comparative Essays* (Gurgaon, Haryana: Three Essays Collective, 2009). *Indians in Kenya: The Politics of Diaspora* is a fair and empathetic account of the sojourn of the Indian diaspora in Kenya. It captures the dynamic and changing political and economic fortunes of Indian settlers in Kenya from the pre-colonial to the post-colonial era.

It examines the different trajectories Indian immigrants faced from their collaboration as part of the British 'subimperialist colonizers' in 1895 to their 'voluntary exodus' from Kenya as non-citizens in 1968. It chronicles the competing, often contradictory, strategies by which the South Asian diaspora sought a political voice in Kenya from the beginning of colonial rule in the late 1890s to independence in the 1960s. *Women, Labour & Politics in Trinidad & Tobago: A History* brings out a lively history of women in the Caribbean and reveals their early feminism and their participation in labour struggles and in radical and liberal political movements by drawing on their rare first-hand testimonies. Their struggles range from the time of slavery and indentureship to national independence in 1962 and the present day. Reddock manifests in her book how gender inequalities have been perpetuated for exploitative ends and explores women's roles and activities in colonial ideology and reality. In his book *Indian Transmigrants*, Ravindra K. Jain pens down essays at various times between 1985 and 2007 to present the historical depth and ethnographic width that are essential to portray and analyse the dynamics of the Indian and, more particularly, Tamilian labour diaspora in Malaysia. Ravindra Jain's empirical studies in this book radiate from the vicissitude of migrants from India to Malaysia on to those in the Caribbean and further on to Australia. His perspective vision encompasses the entire field of modern Indian diaspora. The spectrum of globalization in our times necessitates comparisons over still larger territories. He unravels facets of socio-cultural pluralism, hybridization, ethnic movements, politico-economic mobility and global modernity over a vast territory. Mortan Klass's monograph, *East Indians in Trinidad: A Study in Cultural Persistence*, is a community study emphasizing the continuities that existed in the cultural patterns and institutional structure of second- and third-generation population of East Indians in the Felicity village of central Trinidad with the culture and social structure of eastern India (states of eastern Uttar Pradesh and western Bihar) from where their progenitors came. It provides a sketch of the history of East Indian migration to Trinidad.

In these studies we get a glimpse of the suffering of the migrants at their destination, which is clearly visible in their popular folk culture at the destination.

Most of these works have been conducted in the destination points where the migrants went, and many include folk songs and poetry composed on migration there. However, little work has been done on the effect of migration on the culture of the homeland. This is, in part, explained by the fact that emotions have always seemed tangential (if not fundamentally opposed) to the historical enterprise (Rosenwein

2002: 821). The Bhojpuri folk culture that emerged as an outcome of the sorrow due to the widespread mass migration is still found in this region, and even today the migrants and their families rely on folk culture to release their pent-up sorrow at the separation. Although the destinations have changed, the homeland is still the same, and a study of the folk culture prevalent at the homeland can reveal the continuity and change in the socio-economic and cultural conditions of the people of that region due to the interactions with the migrants who return periodically from their destinations, bringing with them the cultural influences of their destinations, which also influence the original folk culture of the homeland.

Indentured migration turned both the abandoned people in the homeland and those who migrated into 'emotional communities'. At the time when indentured migration took place from the Bhojpuri community, there was a huge exodus of people from the Bhojpuri community. This mass exodus of people caused great cultural pain to the Bhojpuri community and turned the homeland and destination points into an emotional community. The core expression of both the popular culture in the destination and the folk culture in the Bhojpuri region (homeland) is compassion. This expression of compassion not only circulates in the folk culture of both the communities but is also visible in their everyday life, attitudes, behaviour and popular beliefs. Though compassion is a human emotion, the pain and sadness that has arisen due to migration has made this emotion more prominent in the lives of the Bhojpuri men and made them more compassionate and emotional, thereby transforming them into an emotional community. However, it is difficult to quantify or set an indicator for what constitutes an emotional community. The folk cultures of various languages in India have folk songs portraying the *veer ras* (chivalrous) like 'Sahles in Maithili' and 'Ballad of Aalha Udal in Bundelkhand', but the irony is that the Bhojpuri folk culture does not have its own ballad of *veer ras*. We cannot deny the fact that the Bhojpuris have been a warrior class since times immemorial. Thousands of peasants of the Bhojpur area emigrated to the British and Dutch colonies overseas, and these movements must be seen as a continuation of the old military migratory patterns associated with the Bhojpur country for so long (Kolff 1990: 190). It is also interesting to note here that the migrants who went for jobs as soldiers were called *purbiyas* (ibid).

Grierson refers them as a lathi community, but we see that the heroic tales in Bhojpuri folk culture are imbued with the emotion of compassion. In the destinations like Mauritius, Fiji, Trinidad and Guyana, we can find songs of social relations and folk songs full of emotions and compassion more than folk songs that showcase chivalry and gallantry of people.

INTRODUCTION

In other words, we can say that only those folk songs are alive or are being re-created in the diasporic collective memory that directly relate to their pain and suffering. We get descriptions of valour in the proverbs and tales of Bhojpuri folk culture but not in the Bhojpuri folk songs. Mostly there are long compassionate chants when the Bhojpuri songs are sung. All this does not definitively describe an emotional community, but our field studies reveal that pain, suffering and compassion are important elements of folk culture in both the homeland and destination and give rise to an emotional community.

The resulting anguish has been termed *bidesia bhav* (emotionality). The word *bidesia* refers to migrant labourers. The emotions generated because of separation were expressed in the form of literary and cultural expressions like *nautanki* (musical theatre), dramas, folk songs and folk paintings, which led to the emergence of a distinct folk culture in the Bhojpuri region. The *bidesia* folk culture revolves around the theme of the departure of the migrant Bhojpuris and encompasses other similar folk forms on migration popular in the Bhojpuri region like *jantsar* (grind mill songs), *kajri* (seasonal songs), *birha* (song of pain and separation used to be sung by the Ahir caste) and *barahamasi* (songs which constitute suffering of women caused by migration in all the twelve months) within its fold. Parallel to the emerging *bidesia* folk culture developing in India, similar folk cultures were developing in the destination countries. A study of the songs, poetry and literature composed as expressions of grief caused by the separation can shed light on the role of emotions in this process and the depth of sorrow experienced by the two sets of people.

For Bhojpuri people mass-indentured migration was a heavy emotional loss as many tender relationships were torn apart – wives from husbands, sisters from brothers, children from ageing parents. In the emerging folk tradition, the question underlying all songs was *kahe gaile bides* (why did you go overseas?). For various reasons, few of indentured returned. This is why these migrants were addressed as *bidesia*, that is, those who have become foreigners. Since very little folk tradition is written and published, it is difficult to fix the exact time period when it emerged, but in 1858 a prostitute named Sundari, who came to Banaras from Delhi, used the word *bides* as a form of address. Pandit Beni Ram, a resident of Kashi, also composed a folk song that was published in 1884 in which the word *bidesia* was used to address a person who has left and gone away.

The composition of *bidesia* folk songs started around this time and later formed the base for *bidesia* folk culture. In this song, the word *bidesia* is used as a 'tek' for the first time. Scholars believe this is the special and unique feature of the *bidesia* folk tradition.

## INTRODUCTION

The compositions depict the ontology of the pain of the migrants that is centred on separation, due mainly to the need for the money earned by the migrant. People believe most of the time that the root cause of migration of their menfolk, which takes them away from their families and loved ones, is the desire to earn money. The migration, which has been taking place over centuries and is still taking place in contemporary Indian society, is both to foreign lands across the sea and to urban areas inside India. When barter system became outdated and money was accepted as the means of exchange, people from rural society found it difficult to survive and sustain their families. They were thus forced to migrate outside their villages in order to earn money. Money was thus seen as the factor that separated lovers and beloved, wives and husbands, mothers and sons and broke all relationships in the rural society. This is reflected in the folklore created in India both in the past and at present, which describes money as the main cause of migration, whether it is indentured migration or contemporary Middle East migration or internal migration.

Money causes the separation of human relations in two ways – the pull factor and the push factor. Money multiplies our needs. We subsequently require more money to fulfil our ever-growing needs. Since money in the rural economy is less in currency form and flows more in the form of goods, the rural people migrate to cities to earn money for a better living. In this way, money pulls the people towards itself.

In the Bhojpuri folk psyche, money was considered as the factor that caused the separation of the migrants from their families, even though it was poverty that drove the menfolk to leave their families and earn money in other places. Many folk songs narrate this dichotomous perspective towards money in the folk consciousness. The following song is one such example:

> *Railiya bairan more piya ke le jai*
> *Jone sahariya mein piya more naukar*
> *Agiya lage sahar jari jae re*
> *Jone sahibwa ke piya more naukar*
> *Naagin dase sahib mari jae re*
> *Jone tikatwa se piya more jaihain*
> *Pani pare tikat gali jae re*
> *Railiya na bairi se jahajwa na bairi se paisawa bairi na*
> *Mor saiyan ke bilmawe se paiswa bairi na*
>    (sung by Maya Singh aged thirty-eight years,
>         Barwaripur village, Sultanpur district,
>              on 15 November 2013)

In this song, the singer, a woman, is angry that the train has taken her husband away to a big city for work and curses everyone and everything that her husband encounters on the way. She curses the city where her husband is working that it perishes in flame. She curses that a snake stings his boss (sahib) to death, and she also curses that the ticket that he bought for travelling gets soiled in water. However, as her anger ebbs she realizes that it is not the ship or train that is her real enemy but the shortage of money that compels her husband to go to distant places to work and earn money for fulfilling their needs.

Those left behind suffer as much as those who emigrate; hence the wage of migrants is their joint wage. The wives left behind suffer many hardships since they are likely to be ill-treated (regarded as 'widows'), and acquiring the necessities of life may be a struggle, especially when husbands do not send remittances. In the joint family system, a woman expects support from the brothers of her husband and other members of the family, but prolonged absence may put too much strain on the system.

The folk songs concerned with the separation of human bonds are not the mere description of the loneliness of the separated but are also expressions of various social and cultural animosities within and without the family, like intimidation by landlords, moneylenders and *sahukar* (shopkeepers) and the inner-family conflicts in which the wife is dominated by her in-laws. In the folk psyche in the Bhojpuri region, overseas migration was also sometimes perceived as a kind of imprisonment or *kala pani*, which was an island in the Andamans where Indians were imprisoned by the British as it was difficult to escape from there.

Migration was perceived as a kind of punishment for engaging in anti-British activities, and it was a severe punishment inflicted on those accused of treason. Hence, it represented a highly frightening punishment at a distant place from where there would be no news. In Bhojpuri folk consciousness, there is an imagined perception that *kala pani* is located in the East.

### *Bidesia* folk theatre tradition

Another tradition that developed during this period and was part of the same genre was the *bidesia* folk theatre tradition, which was founded by Bhikhari Thakur (1887–1971). In this tradition, the storyline of plays is usually related to the sorrow of a young bride whose husband has been forced to leave her in the village and go to *pardes* or a foreign land to look for work. It develops in the form of Sundari sending a message through a messenger to her husband and telling the messenger to bring him back to the village after releasing him from the clutches of another woman in the city. The story develops in such a fashion that even the most stonehearted person will feel like crying. *Bidesia* theatres were not only about grieving young women but they also narrate the feelings of young men who return to their village searching for work in the city. The plays were based on the *nautanki* style, and all characters, from the king to the yogi, sang and danced on the stage. The characters of the *bidesia* theatre entered the stage singing and then started dancing to the beats of the musical instrument *duggi*. Other musical instruments used included the dholak, sarangi, harmonium, *jhaal, kartal* and *jori*. There were no curtains or stage as the play was performed on benches inside tents or in the open on wooden planks covered with a durrie (rug).

Bhikhari Thakur, popularly known as the 'Shakespeare of Bhojpuri', was also the first person to cast male actors in female roles wearing female clothes. The plays were a mixture of prose and poetry and were filled with *bidesia* songs sung on folk tunes based on *lorikayan, jantsari, sorthi, birha, barahmasa, poorvi, alha, pachra, kunvar bijai, nirgun, chaupai, kavita* and *chaubisa* and other folk songs. Thakur's *bidesia* theatres drew large audiences. His style became so popular that people started calling other *nautankis* also *bidesia* (Narayan 2005: 84–85). The folk genre that developed in the Bhojpuri region at the time when indentured migration took place shows that the going away of migrants resulted in a terrible emotional loss, which was the basis of the *bidesia bhav* that pervaded the entire region.

## Separation and destination

When *bidesia* folk songs reached migrants at their destination points, they too started composing songs as a form of reply to the question 'why did you go overseas?' If the folklore composed in the Bhojpuri region is juxtaposed with the *bidesia* folk songs composed in the colonies, it sounded like an emotional question and answer of this major sociohistorical event. A Fijian folk song narrates the reasons for which the *bidesia* migrant had to leave home:

*Firangi ke rajua maa chhuta mora desua se*
*Gori sarkar chali chal re bidesia*
*Bholi hame dekh arakati bharamaya ho*
*ukalkatta paar jao paanch saal re bidesia*
*Dipua maa lae pakrayo kagadua ho*
*anguthwa lagae dindar re bidesia*
*Paal ke jahajua maa roi dhoi baithi ho*

## INTRODUCTION

*kaise hoi kala pani paar re bidesia*
*jiyara darae ghat kyon nahi aye ho*
*Beete kai din kai maas re bidesia*
*Aai ghat dekhi jab Fijia ke tapua ho*
*Bhaya man hamra udaas re bidesia*
*Kudari kurwal dono hathua mein hamre ho*
*Gham maa pasina bahae re bidesia*
*Khetua mein taas jab deve kulambarwa ho*
*Maar maar hukum chalae re bidesia*
*Kaali kothariya mein beete nahi ratiya ho*
*Kisise batai hum peer re bidesia.*
*Din raat beeti humri dukh mein umariya ho*
*Sukha sab nainwa ke neer re bidesia*
                                    (ibid: 93–95)

*Translation*

The white masters played such a trick on us
that we got separated from our land.
Taking us to be innocent, the *arakati* (dalal) convinced
us to go beyond Calcutta for five years.
He took us to the depot and made us put our thumbprints on the paper.
We sat in the ship with tears in our eyes, wondering how we will undertake such a journey.
The journey is so long that even after many months we have not reached the shore.
When we see the land of Fiji, we felt very sad.
Both *kudari* and 'axe' are in our hands and we are perspiring in the heat.
In the fields, the contractor assigns us a task and makes us do it by force.
It is difficult to spend the night in the dark lodges, and there is no one with whom we can share our pain.
Our life is being spent in this misery, and the tears have dried from our eyes.

In these lines, the *bidesia* is himself narrating the pain and sorrow he feels at being displaced from his homeland. Through such folk songs the migrants themselves agree with the complaints of the Bhojpuri people that they left their homeland in search of money. This is brought out in a Mauritius Bhojpuri folk song:

> *Sonwa karan aili ram, ehire marich des*
> *Segati bhaile sonwa sarir, ehi re marich des*
> (ibid: 96)

> Translation
>
> We came to this land because of money, and this money is the cause of the torture to our bodies.

The *bidesias* themselves say that they did not want to leave their homeland, but compulsions led them to do so. The folk songs sung by the migrants in Suriname depict their misery in their new destinations. These folk songs suggest that the early experience of the *bidesias* was one of sorrow and anguish for their lost country and people (Kamlesh 1999: 99).

These songs reveal the depth of emotional pain or *bidesia bhav* within the indentured migrants who stayed on in their destinations after completing their indentures.

## Missing and searching through letters

The sense of 'disappearance' that occurred during indentured period, due to the lack of awareness of the affected people about their destinations, was the chief reason for the strong emotional base of this kind of migration. They could understand that they were going to Calcutta but found it difficult to understand where they were going from there. Some knew that their loved ones had gone to Suriname, as is evident from the letters that did not reach their destinations and were intercepted by the postal department and have been preserved in the Suriname National Archive, Paramaribo.

These letters reveal the depth of emotional pain within migrants and their loved ones back home. Sadly, there is a cold officious note on them saying that either 'the person named so-and-so of village so-and so in India was not found' or 'the person named so-and-so was not found on the plantation in Suriname named so-and so'. Perusing the contents of these letters shows that most of the letters by family members in India urged migrants to return to India and also emphasized that the money sent by them as remittance was no compensation for their absence. These letters reveal the *bidesia bhav* (emotionality) imbued in the hearts of separated

INTRODUCTION

people. For example, a letter by Shiv Mangal of Asauli village, Ahmadpur, in Raebarelli district of Uttar Pradesh, to his brother Bajrangbali who was working at Sarmacca plantation in Suriname strikingly brings out the emotional pain resulting from separation.

> Greetings to Siddh Sri Sarvoprasayog Bajrangbali from Shivmangal Ram, Suryaram, Bhavani, Gayadin, Gangaprasad and your five nephews and Sevakram, Ramsahai, Bihari, Kairati, Benchu, Chhedi, Mandas, Chandi, Seetal and Bhikhari. May all their 'Ram Ram' (a form of greeting used in rural areas of UP), reach you. Further we are well and we are happy to hear that you are also well. The further news is that please know that we have received Rs. 48 in the month of Kartik. And your mother and sister-in-law and your woman (wife) and your five nephews are all well. You asked about the cultivation so please know that we have a farming of two oxen. By God's grace everything is going well. It is the desire of all of us in the house that you return home. Your mother thinks about you day and night which you should come and see. And we have received the letter which you had sent and have informed about the reply of each person. I don't know whether you will receive it or not.[7]

This letter makes several things clear. Bajrangbali left his wife behind when he emigrated to Suriname. The entire family seems to be missing him and strongly urges him to return. The family, which lived in India around 1901–1902, was a middle class, relatively prosperous family, as they owned two oxen, which were considered a sign of affluence. This raises the question of why Bajrangbali emigrated, if money was not a problem. On the other hand, the family may have benefited from his remittances. Bajrangbali's wife is mentioned marginally while his mother's worry and anxiety is reinforced, probably because at that time women's sexuality was not described although folk songs and oral tradition provided vivid descriptions of the sorrow of forsaken women. The letter was also written by an older brother, who is supposed to maintain a large distance with his younger brother's wife as the relationship entails respect and shame (*lajja*). It is noteworthy that the letter did not reach Bajrangbali but had a note from the emigration office in Paramaribo that they did not find any person by that name at Sarmacca plantation. This could be because he had completed his period of indenture. The emotions hidden in the letter seem to have been waylaid during the journey and are still waiting to reach the person for whom they were intended.

Another letter by Lalbihari to Kunjbihari in Suriname points to three things. The letter urges the migrant to return and specifically requests that he return in Indian clothes and not in Western gear. Kunjbihari seems to have sent a remittance of 110 guilders, which was a large sum at that time, to Lalbihari, which did not reach him. Lalbihari wrote a separate letter to the manager of the plantation where Kunjbihari was working in which he urged him to send Kunjbihari back. He wrote, 'I will pray to God for your well-being for this.' The overriding desire to meet Kunjbihari is evident. This letter too did not reach Kunjbihari. There is a note from the emigration office that no person named Lalbihari was found in the village. In this letter too, the emotions died along with the letter.

The colonial archives in several countries that were the destinations of Bhojpuri migrants contain letters by officers of the immigration department searching for migrants working on plantations in different countries since many of them were untraceable. The large volume of letters in the colonial archives points to the fact that for many in the Bhojpuri region, the story of indenture was one of disappearance and searching for the lost one, and the depth of emotions generated in this process was enormous.

### Plantation life, sense of separation and autobiographical narratives

Literary compositions, including autobiographies written by indentured labourers at their destination points, are another major source for understanding the underlying *bidesia bhav* existing within Bhojpuri migrants. Some of the workers were literate and created compositions such as songs and poems or in very rare cases penned autobiographies describing their lives on the plantations. The depth of their sorrow at leaving their homelands and their loved ones behind is strongly evident in these literary compositions. The compositions of Lalbihari and Munshi Rahman Khan are examples of the *bidesia bhav* that emerge through literature.

Lalbihari, who was born in the Mairatand village in the Chappra district of the Bhojpur region of Bihar, emigrated to Essequibo (British Guiana), where he worked at the Golden Fleece Estate. He published *Damra Fag Bahar* (Holi Songs of Demerara) in 1916. Written in Nagri script, it is a mixture of Bhojpuri and Awadhi collection of original songs for rendition during the Hindu festival of Holi. Lalbihari's works portray the villagization that occurred in the colony. The style of these songs is a mixture of *doha* (couplets), *chaupai* (quatrain), *kabita* (free verse) and *chautal ullara* (rhymes). The collection introduces the author to his audience and relates songs that reveal his contemporary condition and daily life. There are Holi songs expressing the pain of separation as well as bhajans or devotional songs that are philosophical and esoteric prayers. The theme pervading the text is one of anxiety and alienation (*viraha*) (Mohapatra 2004). By adopting the *nirguna* (distinctionless) poetic methods of Kabir and Dadu, Lalbihari spoke of the world of that plantation as an illusory world. The need of money that brought the migrants to *kudesh* (badland) and degraded them into coolies is illusory. He says that all this is very fragile: *Yah sab nahi apnana, Maya jhooth jagat hai sapna* (Don't accept these in your life, illusory falsehood of life is this dream). The author, in fact, advocates a sense of detachment from the surrounding world so that the community can overcome the period of moral degradation forced upon immigrants by the plantation regime (ibid).

The notion of *kudesh* versus *matribhumi* (motherland) is very strong in Lalbihari's compositions. Separation from *matribhumi* is expressed as *viraha* for the homeland. Lalbihari says when he enlisted as a coolie he was bereft of *dharma* (duty) and *vivek* (conscience). Bihari said that he had come for *naukri* (work) and not to be reduced to a 'coolie'. He describes the drudgery of everyday life, drawing parallels with his homeland. The narration about his motherland is always positive, as he remembers his family and village life. He contemplates his life in a better country and laments how the poor are deceived and tricked to immigrate to *kudesh*. In the final section, the author contemplates as to how to carry on the back-breaking drudgery for five long years, worrying about his eligibility for a ticket (read passage) of leave from the plantation. The passage of time on the plantation and constant anxiety lead some to renounce material life and become seers (*sadhu, fakir*), while others wander about in deep distress and agonizing anxiety, wondering how to carry on with what they regard as their doomed lives. The section ends with advice to indentured labourers to be patient. They should remain on plantations, like the village back home, under the benign guidance of their *sardars* (leaders, elders). Even while allowing for nostalgia, the writing points to the emotional aspects of separation and the pain associated with the process.

Munshi Rahman Khan (1874–1972) was an educated Muslim youth who became prey to the diabolical plans of two Muslim men. A young lad in his mid-20s, he was tricked by them as they promised him a 'government job'. Though his indentured labour period expired after five years, Khan remained in Suriname to become an independent agriculturist and lived in the country until his death. He kept a diary that provides a glimpse into the life and times of migrant coolies. He subsequently became a prolific writer, and his autobiography, *Jeevan Prakash* (*Life's Light*), gives us a unique insight into the history of the indentured labourers in the Caribbean. Through such literary and cultural productions, we see that the immigrants were remembering at the destination what they had left behind. Even if they were materially better off, they were critiquing their everyday lives in the new setting. While the labour regime attempted to transform them into colonial subjects (migrants), *bidesia bhav* appeared as a subversive feeling and they contested the colonial *bhav* by remembering their deserted families, their beloved ones, and the homeland.

## Indentured subjectivity and *bidesia bhav*

While there is an assumption that the indentured were of the lowest castes and lacked any education, the many individual biographies that have been unearthed in various receiving colonies show that there were a fair number of semi-educated and reasonably well-off individuals. Perhaps they hoped to obtain, or were promised, positions in the civil service in the colonies. It must have come as a huge shock when they discovered that they were destined to work as 'coolies' on the sugarcane plantations where they faced harsh living conditions and were forced to perform hard manual labour by their overseers. The various Coolie Ordinances passed after 1840, and consolidated in the late 1890s as Immigration Ordinance of British Guiana (1893) and Trinidad (1899), regulated every aspect of the working and, to a large extent, non-working lives of the immigrants (such as marriages, festivals, sickness, housing and return to India).

The technicians and managers who ran the plantations modelled them on the slave plantation with its rigid labour discipline and their belief in European racial superiority. Thus a complete and systematic system of subjugation of the indentured was put in place. This dichotomy between what they found in their destinations and what they had left behind in their homelands was the basis of the *bidesia bhav*, which emerged in the psyche of migrants, since at their workplaces they had to work as coolies while in their imagination they were still in their homelands. In order to narrow the gap between their imagination and reality, migrants struggled to rebuild their broken world to make it as close to home as possible. Their collective memory and cultural heritage worked hand in hand in reshaping a new world that matched their own culture. Since the complete reconstruction of their old world was not possible, they re-created aspects of their culture that were allowed by the Dutch, such as celebrating local festivals.

When indentured migrants left their native lands, they took their cultural 'baggage' that included both intangible artefacts and tangible artefacts, in order to keep the cultural link (Majumder 2010: 12). The Hindus were given twenty-two and Muslims sixteen recognized religious days. On these days, they celebrated their respective festivals with great enthusiasm and enjoyment, which helped them to maintain ties with their religion and culture, and unburdened their discontent outside of these festivals. The new generations also retained the vernacular language since the Dutch did not impose the Dutch language on the immigrants and introduced special schools on several plantations where the native language was taught. The contestations between the conditions faced by immigrants at work and their imagination and the negation of the coolie status were an essential part of *bidesia bhav*, which sprouted in colonial sugar plantations among Bhojpuri migrants.

## Contemporary migration from the Bhojpuri region

The Bhojpuri region from where the maximum colonial migration took place is a cultural and linguistic region that covers parts of Bihar and East Uttar Pradesh. Some of the districts lying in this region from where most migration took place were Sultanpur, Faizabad, Barabanki, Lucknow, Hardoi, Pratapgarh, Bhojpur, Sasaram and Buxar, Azamgarh and so on. As per the sixty-fourth round survey on Employment and Unemployment and Migration Particulars by National Sample Survey Organization 2007–2008, 29 per cent of Indian population was migrants with significant rural–urban and male–female differentials.[8] Out of 1,000 persons, 189 persons from Bihar and 256 from the state of Uttar Pradesh are migrating from rural areas. Similarly, for urban Bihar and Uttar Pradesh, the migration rates are 345 and 310 persons, respectively, per 1,000 consecutively. The distribution of migrants by the nature of movements shows that migration in the states of Bihar and Uttar Pradesh was mostly of permanent type, with 941 and 931 persons per 1,000, respectively, migrating from the states of Bihar and Uttar Pradesh consecutively.

Although the following generations of the migrants from the Bhojpuri region who left Indian shores in the colonial period are now leading affluent lives and are in good economic condition, the people who are living in these regions at present are still leading miserable and poverty-stricken lives as little economic development has taken place since the colonial migrants left. This poor economic condition is still compelling lakhs of youths to migrate to cities like Delhi, Mumbai, Calcutta, Surat or those in Assam and Punjab, where they work as labourers, auto and cab drivers, roadside vendors and so on. Each day at least a hundred people gather at the railway station or bus depot in these places and reach the closest railway junctions like Allahabad, Banaras, Katihar, Barauni, Samastipur, Mokama, Patna, Buxar, Ara, Sasaram, Muzaffarpur, Chhapra and Siwan, which lie on the route of long-distance trains.

## INTRODUCTION

Unfortunately, although the migrants leave their homelands to escape from penury and misery, their condition in the big cities where they go to in search of a better-living condition is extremely pathetic and they face similar oppression and exploitation that their ancestors faced in the colonial period. They are derogatorily referred to as *bhaiyas* (big brother), and so the trains that carry these contemporary migrants can be called *bhaiya* express, metaphorically signifying trains that convey migrants. Most of the migrants are recruited by labour contractors who beg or cajole, lure or threaten them to go to work in factories in big cities where labour is needed. These labour contractors are the modern-day equivalents of the recruiters or *arkatiyas* (middlemen) of the colonial times who used to travel from village to village, luring hapless innocent people into subdepots and depots, to be later taken to work as '*girmitia* (agreement) labourers' in colonial overseas plantations. Hardly any of the migrants are aware of their destination and are completely dependent on the labour contractors to take them to their work places. Few migrants take their families with them when they go outside the village for work. Thus the women, children and other family members remain in the village, while the men stay away for eight months to one year and then return for a few months only to go back again.

It is interesting to note that the *bidesia* folk culture that emerged in the colonial period is still present in the Bhojpuri region today and even now both the migrants and their families take recourse to folk culture in the form of folk songs to express their sorrow at the separation. After a hard day's gruelling labour when they get together in their slums or ghettoes and sing songs together, they are able to mitigate some of the pain at separating from their native villages and loved ones. For the people who are left behind in the homeland too, like the wives, children, parents and siblings, this cultural repertoire provides solace and helps them to surmount the pain and anguish at the going away of their loved one. Thus the repertoire of cultural forms is still alive in the folk memory and popular culture of Bhojpuri people though the form has changed with new technological developments and the onset of modernity.

While the migrants from the Bhojpuri region who went overseas were referred to as *bidesia*, the present-day migrants who migrate to big cities within India are referred to as *pardesi* (a migrant returning to his homeland). The present-day Bhojpuri folk culture can thus be called the *pardesia* folk culture, which is an offshoot of the *bidesia* folk culture. The songs and poems that are composed by the Bhojpuri migrants (*pardesis*) at their destination points in Surat, Delhi or Mumbai include all the new experiences that they make during their stay there although the bedrock of these new compositions is the original culture that they grew up with.

INTRODUCTION

When they return to their villages for their annual visits, the new experiences made by them are shared with the people back home, which are then woven into the folk tradition in their native places. The folk culture of the Bhojpuri region is thus constantly changing and evolving even though the thread of continuity, which is the emotion produced by the separation, is still running through it. In the recent past many commercial poets and songwriters have emerged both in the Bhojpuri region and in the destination points who compose songs and poems based on the theme of separation and sell them in the form of booklets and CDs to the migrants. In addition, many professional theatre companies stage theatres around this theme, which people at both the places flock to see. Bhojpuri channels like Mahua, ETV Bihar and ETV Uttar Pradesh also telecast several serials and soaps whose pegs are the theme of separation, which are very popular among Bhojpuri viewers. Thus the *pardesi* culture has become extremely vibrant and has also become greatly commercialized since the companies producing this culture have understood its tremendous market potential due to the strong emotion underlying it, but a great deal is still in the oral form among the ordinary people living in villages and slums.

## Organization of the book

This book will focus on the migrants who went from the Bhojpuri[9] region of northern India to the Dutch colony of Suriname between 1873 and 1916 (De Klerk 1953) to work on the Caribbean country's sugar, coffee, cotton and cocoa plantations. Many of the indentured remained in Suriname after completing their indentures, and their descendants underwent a second migration when they moved to Holland after the Surinamese independence in 1975. Thus, there is a common cultural heritage among people in these three regions of the world. Even though these Hindi-speaking people of Indian origin have become part of the native population of these countries, they have preserved the folk dialect–mixed Hindi language and culture and religion, though they have imbibed host countries' culture and language through acculturation. In addition this book will study and document the folk culture of the Bhojpuri region of India from where large-scale migration is still taking place. This study of the flow of cultural productions in the past and the present will create a holistic picture of the migration from the Bhojpuri region over the years through the folk culture of this region. As a part of this endeavour, the book will also address the formations of cultures in the process of identity-making of the approximately 20 crore Bhojpuri speakers scattered all over the world. Thus the book will tell the story of the continuum of long-term migration from the Bhojpuri region through folk culture. The range of the book covers migration from Bhojpuri region from the colonial to the contemporary period. It will be developed through archival records; secondary literature; oral interviews in villages of the Bhojpuri region, Suriname, the Netherlands, Mumbai, Surat, Ghaziabad and other places related with Bhojpuri migration; and a large collection of folk songs of migration in the homeland and destinations.

The book will be organized into the following chapters.

Chapter 1, 'Who migrated and why: the *bidesia* story', will describe the journey of the migrants from the subdepots to Suriname. After being recruited by recruiters from their villages, migrants were first taken to the subdepots located in various places in Uttar Pradesh and Bihar where they had to spend a few days in virtual imprisonment so that they could not run away back to their villages. When a good number of people had been collected, they were taken by train to the main depot in Calcutta from where they would be shipped overseas to various British, Dutch and French colonies in Mauritius, Suriname, Fiji, Guyana and so on. The potential migrants had to stay in Calcutta depot for a long time till more migrants had been brought in by recruiters from other places. They were kept under the supervision of guards and watchmen who worked under orders from colonial officers. At the depot and before embarking the ship, the potential migrants were enlisted and made to sign an agreement that they were going as indentured labourers through their own choice for a period of five years. The overseas ship journey took several months, and after a long gruelling journey the migrants reached Suriname where they were made to settle in the colonial plantations. At the end of the indentureship period, many migrants who had married other women migrants by then preferred to settle in Suriname with their families where they were given land and money by the government.

Chapter 2 will describe the various phases in the settlement history of the Bhojpuri migrants in Suriname. These phases are indentureship (1873–1921), post-indentureship (1921 present), reconstruction (1921–1945), modernization (1945–1975) and independence and the second wave of diaspora (1975–present).

Chapter 3 will provide an emotional history of the exile and separation of the Bhojpuri migrants from India to Suriname and then to the Netherlands, which gave rise to the *bidesia bhav* (emotionality).

Chapter 4 will give an overview of the *bidesia* folk culture. We will first describe the *bidesia* folk culture in India, with special emphasis on *bidesia nautanki* and its composer Bhikhari Thakur. Next we will describe the *bidesia* folk culture in Suriname, which was the folk culture that developed parallel to the *bidesia* folk culture in India. While most of the folk culture in India posed the underlying question to the migrants '*Kahe gaile bides:* Why did you go overseas?', the *bidesia* folk culture in Suriname in songs and literature was in the form of answers in which the migrants tried to justify why they migrated and left behind their native places and loved ones. Thus if the two folk cultures are analysed they will appear to be questions and answers. In this chapter we will also describe the Hindustani music that developed in Suriname known as *baithak-gana* (a form of singing popular among Surinamese Hindustanis in Suriname) and also the Indo-Surinamese drama. Later when the Hindustani Surinamese migrated to the Netherlands, they further developed the *baithak-gana* tradition there, which we will also describe in this chapter. In addition, we will describe the Hindustani Surinamese language known as *Sarnami*, which is an amalgamation of Bhojpuri, Dutch, Creole and so on. The language has now developed its own literature, and it is being further expanded in the Netherlands by the present generations of Dutch Hindustani.

Chapter 5 will describe the mass migration that is still going on from the Bhojpuri region to various parts of India, especially to big cities like Delhi, Mumbai, Surat and Bangalore. Due to the absence of viable and sustainable livelihood opportunities in their native places, the youth are forced to migrate in large numbers to seek their fortunes in other parts of India, and the long-distance trains from the closest junction stations are filled to capacity by mostly illiterate and unskilled youths. *Bhaiya* express is the metaphorical name given to these trains since most of the migrants are derogatorily addressed as *bhaiyas* in their destination points, and in this chapter we will describe a journey to Mumbai, Surat and Ghaziabad by *bhaiya* express. In addition, we will include narratives of separation from some of the migrants and their family members.

Chapter 6 will provide a documentation of the cultural productions generated in the Bhojpuri region due to migration that were produced in the colonial period and are still present there.

Chapter 7 will describe how migrants are being used by various political parties in the destination points to win votes as they constitute a large vote bank, and how cultural productions based on migration and separation are used to emotionally win them over. Cultural productions based on the themes of migration and separation are also used by political leaders in the Bhojpuri region to win the votes of the people as migration is a burning issue there, with almost every family having some members who have migrated, and people are emotionally touched by this theme.

In the end, we will present the Conclusion.

## Notes

1 http://www.scribd.com/doc/43336905/Hybridity-by-Homi-Bhabha#scribd.
2 Field documentation by Jai Prakash Tripathi and Archana Singh, village Baderi, Jaunpur district, Uttar Pradesh, dated 17 October 2015.
3 PP 1910 XXVII (ed. 5192), PI 1, p. 18.
4 Stearns and Stearns, *Anger*, 249, n.31; 12 ('common folk'); 16 ('middle-class Protestants').
5 PP 1910 XXVII (ed. 5192).
6 *Kahe Gaile Bides: Why Did You Go Overseas?* Resource book of the Bidesia Project (2005–2007), pp. 21–22.
7 A letter written by Shiv Mangal of Asauli village, Ahmadpur, in district Raebarelli of Uttar Pradesh, to his brother Bajrangbali who was working in Sarmacca plantation in Suriname. National Archive, Paramaribo.
8 NSS Report No. 533: Migration in India: July 2007–June 2008.
9 This included people from the Braj, Awadh and Magahi regions of Bihar and Uttar Pradesh.

# 1

## WHO MIGRATED AND WHY

### The *bidesia* story

*Piya Chawle Pardes, Bhejle Pati Na Sandes*
*Mora Jia Mein Anes Sunu Mori Sajni*
(My husband has gone to *pardes* and has not sent me any message. My heart is filled with worry, O friend.)

(Bhairo)
(Singh 1958: 190)

The key persons in the migration story were the *arkatiyas* or recruiters of Indian labourers to work in the sugar plantations of Suriname, Mauritius and other European colonies. They were the Indian middlemen or commission agents who were hired by Indian sub-agents, who in turn were hired by an emigration agent, kept in Calcutta by the Dutch government for recruiting Indian immigrants for Suriname. William Frank Dowson, a partner of the house of Messrs Heoley, Dowson and Co., an emigrant agent company for exporting coolies from India to overseas colonies, revealed during the course of an interrogation by the committee appointed by the Supreme Government of India to enquire into the abuses alleged to exist in exporting coolies and Indian labourers of various classes from Bengal Hill to other countries[1] that it was a highly organized system that started around 1833 when the first overseas migration from the Bhojpuri region took place. The superior native agents were paid Rs 200–500 to defray the expenses of the coolies in mofussil areas. The commission per coolie varied from Rs 10 to 30 per man, and in cases where the agents made advance payment the commission was Rs 30. The amount paid to the native agents was usually given back since the native agents derived their profit from the coolies themselves who paid them at the rate of Rs 5 per man from the advance payment of six months given to them. The committee was appointed five years after the first ship left with immigrants, and it not only looked into the abuses but also looked into the method of recruitment of labourers in the homeland. Dowson, himself an emigration agent, admitted that the system was a vicious one, but was also very lucrative.

The *arkatiyas* were the direct recruiters of Indian labourers who had a wide network in the villages and kasbahs of North India and operated during feasts, melas, open-air traditional shows, pilgrimages and so on, where a large number of people used to gather. These *arkatiyas* also operated from railway stations where they were known to kidnap hapless young men and send them to far-off places across the sea (Majumder 2010: 19).

Etymologically, the word *arkatiya* may be derived from the word *katiya* meaning 'bait', since they baited the recruitees with their smooth talks. The most important attribute of these *arkatiyas* was their smooth tongue by which they used to entice candidates by telling them wonderful stories about the bounteous and plentiful life in a place that could be reached by sea. They would paint a rosy picture of the place, promising that they would be able to excavate gold from the gold mines existing there. They would pronounce the names of the places in such a manner that the candidate would think that it was somewhere close by and had strong links with Hindu mythology. For example, Suriname was pronounced as 'Sri Ram tapu', which aroused the idea that it was the land where Sri Ram lived. Most of these persons had never ever left their villages and had little idea about life outside. They were thus highly suggestible, which made them easy preys to the sales talks of the *arkatiyas*. They thus allowed themselves to go voluntarily since both at the subdepot and at the main depot the newcomer was asked whether he was leaving India voluntarily or not (ibid: 19–20).

The manner in which candidates were recruited by *arkatiyas* can be understood from the documentation of Munshi Rahman Khan, mentioned by Gautam (1995), who was taken to Suriname in the early twentieth century. Khan was an educated person who had studied to be a munshi. He was working as a teacher in a middle school in Maudha when he went to Chandpur to visit an uncle's house. From there he decided to go to Kanpur to see a Ram Lila show. Before leaving for Kanpur, he was warned by his uncle to be careful since he had heard that many people were being kidnapped by certain people called *arkatiyas* who were sending them off to far-off islands. To this Khan replied that he was an educated man and would not be entrapped by their sweet talks (ibid: 21).

After spending a few days in Kanpur, when he was returning to the Kanpur railway station, he was stopped by two gentlemen who greeted him and asked him where he was heading for in such a hurry. On replying that he was returning to his village they told him that he seemed to be an educated person and would be better off working as a sardar in a sugar plantation. Khan became convinced by their glib tongue and allowed himself to be taken to a subdepot in Kanpur. After spending some time in the subdepot when the number of recruitees had reached sixty, he was sent with a group to Faizabad to another subdepot. There he stayed with the group for another three weeks. Khan narrates that while in Faizabad one of the persons of the group ran away across the Saryu River to Lakkarmandi. Khan was sent to bring him back. This incident shows that not every recruit was convinced by the sweet talks of the recruiters and motivated enough to go away to a far-off land. Many of them were also missing their wives and families and were longing to go back to them. Thus there were multiple ambiguities existing in the minds of people of the region about the overseas migration. Some went willingly to the depot with the *arkatiya* in the hope of getting a well-paid job, but after seeing the hard life at the depots they were disillusioned and wanted to leave. Others were willing to accept the hard life at the depot in the hope of the good prospects in the future. Many, who had been forcibly trapped, searched for an opportunity to run away (ibid: 21–22). In the entire Bhojpuri region at large also, there was a fear psychosis among the people that some smooth-talking persons called *arkatiyas* kidnapped men. This can be discerned from the narrative of Khan who wrote that his uncle had warned him that certain well-dressed persons were on the prowl to take people to far-off lands (Gautam 1995).

The *arkatiyas* presented an image of being gentlemen with well-starched clothes. They looked *sharif* (gentlemen), as mentioned by Khan. Often unfair means were also used by them since each recruit was worth a good sum of money. According to a report of a committee appointed by the Supreme Government of India to enquire into the abuses alleged to exist in exporting Indian labourers, which was placed in the British Parliament, the coolies were often exported by fraud and misrepresentation. Munshis or *daffadars* (a rank equivalent to sergeant in the cavalry of the British Indian Army), who were another kind of commission agents, induced them to come to Calcutta by persuading them that they would be given employment as peons under the company, to work on the public roads or as gardener, labourers and so on. What the system followed was that the *daffadars* went to the country, met people there and enticed them with promises of service, promising the upcountry men the services of porter (*durwan*) and the others work as labourers in Calcutta. They used to be brought to the city and kept waiting until they became impatient and asked for service. The *daffadars* then told them that they were sorry but the service they thought for them could not be obtained. Then when the coolies were about to go away, the *daffadar* told them to either pay him for his service or else go overseas.[2]

In the imagination of local people, recruiters were looked upon as schemers, liars and also kidnappers. They recruited people by giving them the wrong idea that they could return home for the weekend, promised easy work, inflated the wages the recruits would receive and painted a picture of a land filled with milk and honey. Chance encounters with strangers were discouraged in most households in the Bhojpuri region since the strangers exploited the misfortune of people and recruited them for migration. A narrative by Baba Ambika Sarju throws light on the modus operandi of recruiters. Sarju is a hundred-year-old Bhojpuri migrant who was transported to Suriname in 1912. He belonged to Raebareli and his father's name was Sarju. The name of the ship on which he, along with the other indentured labourers, travelled to Suriname was called *Matla Jahaj, Dui Lumber* (Matla Ship No. 2) (Majumder 2010: 29).

The dishonesty of recruiters is also documented in colonial records, which validate the image of recruiters in the common imagination of the people. Many recruiters had their licenses revoked for various reasons like carelessness in the recruitment and registration of female emigrants, forcibly recruiting women against their wishes and making false statements while doing registration (Bahadur 2013: 38). Sometimes they forcibly made women spend the night outside their homes, and in the morning when they felt dishonoured and could not return to their father's or husband's homes they were taken to recruitment centres to be sent overseas (ibid: 39).

## Subdepot, train and journey to Calcutta

While many subdepots were scattered throughout North India located in key centres such as Allahabad, Kanpur, Lucknow, Faizabad, Banaras, Ghazipur and Buxar, the main 'coolie depot' was opened in Garden Reach on the banks of the River Hooghly in Calcutta. The subdepots were run by the sub-agents. At that time the labourers were transported to depots by both passenger trains and goods trains. The railway network had not been expanded, and trains travelled only short distances. In the first phase of laying railway tracks under the East Indian Railway in 1853, trains moved only between Calcutta to Mirzapur. Trains ran up to

*Figure 1.1* Travelling Coolies. Photograph: Ds P.M. Legene 1914. Collection Tropenmuseum 60048465

Bharwari station to carry materials to lay tracks, and construction work was in progress when the 1857 rebellion started. After peace was established, on 3 March 1856, train movement started from Prayag to Kanpur, but because there was no bridge across the Yamuna, trains used to run only up to the Allahabad fort. After the Tons Bridge was constructed in April 1864, trains started going on the other side of Mirzapur. Since 15 August 1865, when the Yamuna Bridge was constructed in Allahabad, trains started running up to the main station. In 1863 the line between Naini and Jabalpur opened, and in 1903 the railway line up to Bombay via Cheoki was opened. In 1905 the second line from Allahabad to Faizabad was opened, for which another bridge near Phaphamau was constructed. In 1922 a small railway line between Prayag and Banaras was built by Bengal North Western Railway, and for this a bridge was built across Ganga in Daraganj (Srivastava 1937: 202). Mr Legene, who was working in Suriname as a manager in a sugar plantation, once visited India and took some photographs of the lifestyle and migration process. One photograph contained in his family photo album gives a glimpse of a migrant's journey to a depot, which shows a big open goods train with labourers piled into the bogies. The coolies have *muretha* (turban) tied around their heads, wearing long kurtas (shirts) and loin cloth up to their knees. Some of them also have a cloth wrapped around them. Some have long sticks with them. The women have their heads covered with their dhotis.[3]

A glimpse of the tidal wave of the migration process can be obtained from the description of folklorist Ramnaresh Tripathi who used to travel from place to place collecting folklores. He writes,

> I was travelling from Jaunpur to Prayag. At Bhannor station, I saw some women probably belonging to the Ahir or Chamar communities, who had come see off some males and a few females at the station, weeping loudly. The train started moving, leaving the weeping women behind. By coincidence the men going to Calcutta were in the bogie in which I was travelling. With them there were three or four women who were also going to Calcutta. As soon as the train started moving they started singing and crying. I recorded the song being sung by them (Majumder 2010: 22). It went like this:

*Puruba se aai reliya pachhun se jahajiya*
*Piya ke ladi lei gai ho.*
*Reliya hoi gai mor sabatiya piya ke ladi lei gai ho*
*Reliya na bairi jahajiya na bairi uhai paiswai bairi ho*
*Deswa deswa bharmaiwai uhai paiswai bairi ho*
*Bhukhiya na laagai piasiya na laagai humke mohiya lagai ho*
*Tohri dekhike suratiya humke mohiya laagai ho*
*Ser bhar gohuwa baris din khaibai piya ke jaibe na debe ho*
*Rakhbe ankhiya hajurwan piya ke jai na debai ho.*[4]

*Translation*

The train came from the east and the ship came from the west and took my husband away.
Railway has become my co-wife who has taken my husband away.
Rail is not my enemy, ship is not my enemy, money is my enemy which makes my husband go from country to country.
I have no hunger, I have no thirst, I feel very loving towards him.
When I see his face I feel very affectionate.
I will make one seer of wheat last one year but I won't let my husband go away.
I will keep him in front of my eyes and not let him go away.

The journey of a migrant from his village in the Bhojpuri region till the dockyard at Calcutta can be observed from the vivid narrative of

Munshi Rahman Khan. He narrates that after spending some weeks at the depot at Kanpur he was sent to a depot in Faizabad where ninety more immigrants joined. From Faizabad via Lucknow and Mughalsarai, they were taken to Calcutta after a two-day train journey. During the train journey through the Bhojpur region, batches of immigrants were put on the train at various stations where the subdepots were located. During the train journey no one was allowed to go out without the permission of the watch keepers. At the Howrah railway station, the group was received by the Bengali workers of the Calcutta depot. They took the immigrants in batches of six persons in small boats to the Garden Reach depot (Majumder 2010: 23).

From the description of Khan it appears that there was a sardar or *jamadar* (the headman) who received the immigrants and looked after them. A strict vigilance was kept on them so that no one could escape. Most of the immigrants were farmers, but there were also smiths, barbers, weavers, carpenters, shoemakers, dhobis (washermen), shopkeepers and also educated people like teachers who were recruited to work as supervisors or sardars. Since no high-caste Brahmins were allowed to immigrate as they were considered too soft to do manual work, many Brahmins changed their name by dropping their surnames and giving up their religious symbols like the *janeu* (sacred thread, which is a sign of Brahmins). After arriving in Calcutta, the emigrants were made to strip their clothes and were given soap to bathe in the Hooghly. Many high-caste Brahmins used to slip off their sacred threads and floated them down the Hooghly (Bahadur 2013: 43). The stay in the depot disintegrated all caste and religious boundaries, and each person acquired only one identity that was 'coolie'. The food served to the migrants was another way by which caste and religious identities broke since both vegetarian and nonvegetarian food was served at the depot and all the coolies had to eat together violating caste and religious rules.[5]

Before the journey, the immigrants had to undergo a thorough medical check-up to ensure that their health was good. They were also issued clothes that were in accordance with the weather in the countries where they were migrating and were identical like a uniform. People migrating to Suriname were given a uniform kit consisting of one tin plate, one tin water container, two blankets (one red cotton and the other black woollen, three kurtas – one red, one black and the other printed), two dhotis, two caps (one black and the other printed) and a big bag to keep all these items (Tiwari *et al.* 2005: 65). Those who were migrating to West Indies were given clothes suitable for the cold weather prevailing around Africa's southern tip. The women were allotted two flannel jackets, a woollen petticoat and worsted stockings as well as a sari, while men were allotted wool trousers, a red woollen cap and a jacket. Sometimes they were given dhotis instead of trousers (Bahadur 2013: 44; see also Prakash 2006).

The migrants who had been recruited often stayed in the depot for more than a month till the requisite number of migrants per ship had been recruited and brought to the depot. Munshi Rahman Khan narrates that just before the departure of the ship there were mixed feelings among the immigrants. There was a sort of commotion of joy, fear and anger. A few immigrants could not eat and a few could not sleep. For some it was the last day to be with the mother country, while for others it was an opportunity to become rich. They all knew that the coming years were going to be very hard (Gautam 1995; see also Prakash 2006).

### *Bidesia* in ship

The movement of the migrants by train to their depots was not as much of a trauma as the moment when they embarked on the ship. For most of them the feeling of separation from their homeland hit them sharply as soon as they stepped on to the ship. While some of the migrants were excited thinking of the new life they would be experiencing, many of them felt that they were being exiled to a far-off place where they would be totally cut off from their families. This feeling also led many migrants to revolt and try to jump off the ship. During the interrogation of Mr J.H. Patton, the magistrate of 24 Pergunnahs, Bengal, while compiling the report on the abuses committed on the coolies being sent to Mauritius, he revealed that he released twenty-six men who were shipped on board the *Edward*. He said, 'One man named Bhahadoor, a tall athletic Coolie compelled the captain of the small vessel taking the coolies to the ship, to go to land. The moment they reached shore, all the coolies jumped overboard.' The Emigration Officer Mr Browne called on Mr Patton the next day and asked him to let the coolies go on board the next day, but all the coolies expressed their unwillingness to go, so they were not sent (Majumder 2010: 25–26).[6]

The suffering that the migrants experienced on being separated from their near and dear ones was equally shared by the family members who were left behind. This pain was a constant companion of the migrants. It travelled with them on the ship and remained constantly with them in the land of exile. This pain was experienced with equal intensity by the family members who were left behind, and this can be evidenced from the folklores composed by a singer called Sundar. Sundar was a court singer who came to Banaras from Delhi after the revolt of 1857 when the court was disintegrated. She settled down in Banaras and composed many songs there. Many of them depict the pain of separation of men and women when the men are exiled to a far-off place, also referred to as *kala pani*.

One such song is as follows:

> *Are rama nagar naiyya jala kalapaniyan re hari*
> *Sabhke ta naiyya jala kasi ho bisesar rama*
> *Nagar naiyya jala kalapaniyan re hari*
> *Gharawa mein rowen nagar bhai o bahiniyan rama*
> *Sejiya pe rowe bari dhaniya re hari*
> (Sundar [vaishya])<br/>(Singh 2001: 153)

*Translation*

Hey Rama Nagar's boat is going to *kala pani* O Hari.
Everyone's boat goes to Kasi or Bisesar, Rama.
But Nagar's boat is going to *kala pani*, O Hari.
In his house weep Nagar's brothers and sisters, Rama.
On his bed weeps his wife, O Hari.

Munshi Rahman Khan in his memoirs has also vividly described his journey by ship to Suriname. He says that the name of his ship was *Avon* and was the fortieth ship to sail to Suriname, the first being *Lalla Rookh* that had sailed in 1873. Khan's ship had three masts, and its captain was J. Burley. It was very big and had a lot of facilities such as a hospital, cooking facilities, latrines, good drinking water and a lot of fresh cool air (ventilation). According to the description, there were 750 people on board, but following the colonial report of 1898 the number of immigrants who went to Suriname was only 618. Out of this group two babies were born on the ship and four had died during the voyage. Most of the immigrants were not only farmers, but also smiths, barbers, weavers, carpenters, shoemakers, dhobis (washermen), shopkeepers and three teachers. There were also many small children. Khan writes that there were 150 *habshis* (blacks) who were the workers in the ship. There were also a few immigrants who had already returned to India after their indenture contract but had again decided to go to Suriname for a new contract. The spoken language of the immigrants with the officers and workers of the ship was Hindi (Majumder 2010: 26).

During the sea voyage when the sea became rough most of the time people were not to be seen on the deck but were on their beds. Many were ill and vomiting. The ship took four weeks to reach Cape Town in Africa. At Cape Town and St Helena the ship took new provision, freshwater and food. From Cape Town to St Helena the ship took two more months. When the *Avon* left St Helena, a storm hit the ship. All the passengers were asked to go down from the upper deck. The blow of the storm was so strong that the ship workers were asked to lower down the masts. One of the masts was broken and was thrown into the sea. It took two hours for the storm to subside (ibid: 26).

Khan writes that the food served on the ship was better than that served at the Calcutta depot. It consisted of rice, dhal, vegetables, tamarind sauce, tin meat and lemon juice. On three days of the week, rice was served; on the next three days roti was served, and on Sunday *bhuja* (snack) was served. Fresh sheep was served every two weeks. At St Helena, the captain distributed pears to each migrant (Gautam 1995).

From the examination of a sardar named Ramdeen and six coolies originally from Banaras, Gaya and Serampore on 10 December 1840, it is clear that the coolies had very little money when they went, although the contractors claimed that they were given some advance before leaving India. They only had a set of clothes and a *lota* (small round metal pot). Ramdeen, the sardar, who looked after twenty coolies under him, narrated that they were in great distress on board the ship for want of water. Four times he himself paid a rupee for each *lota* of water. They were also not given enough to eat and had to bribe the serang to give them more, with the money they had been given as six months' advance. The dhal and the rice were mixed up and served, and they were given only about three-eighths of a seer a day. The officer of the ship used to call them to pull the ropes. Those who went were ill-treated, but others who said that this was not a part of their agreement and refused had their blankets and clothes snatched away and thrown overboard (Majumder 2010: 27).[7] The condition of the immigrants was extremely pathetic by the time they reached their destination. A medical report of a committee set up in Guyana said that 'there were many weedy, and of poor physique, and a large proportion of sickly ones' (Bahadur 2013: 55). Often epidemics struck in the ships, claiming many lives during the journey. Many of the immigrants were not given enough food on the ship and looked starved when they reached the port. The government was paid two-thirds of the passage money by planters who employed the immigrants after their arrival, and often their arrival was kept a secret for a week and a half. During this period they were put on a diet of cod liver oil and iron to build up their strength so that the planters would not refuse to employ weak and starved labourers (ibid: 55).

The journey by ship was a grim foreboding of the misfortune awaiting the coolies in the colonial plantations. There was also a deep sense of apprehension, anxiety and fear among them about the life awaiting them. Being drastically cut off from their homeland and their near and dear ones, the memory of their loved ones was the only thing that kept their bodies and minds together. The only means by which they sustained themselves from this intense emotional loss was their cultural baggage of folk music, songs and folk cultural memories that they had carried with them far away across the oceans. The common sorrow of all the migrants, however, forged emotional bonds between the migrants that gave birth to different kinds of identities. For example the migrants who had been together in the same subdepot and depot called each other *dipua bhais* (men who migrated from the same depot which were constituted for appointing indentured migrants during colonial times) or *dipua bahens* (women). The migrants who had travelled on the same ship called each other *jahaji bhais* (ship brothers) or *jahajiyas* (ship brothers), while the migrants who had sailed from the port in Kolkata (Calcutta) were referred to as *kalkattiyas* (the migrants who went through Calcutta port) at the destination. These new identities, that is *dipua, jahajiya* and *kalkattiya*, transcended the barriers of language, caste and religion and built up long-lasting bonds of love and friendship, which sustained them over the years of separation from their own family members (Majumder 2010: 28–29).

## Notes

1 Emigration Debate in British Parliament: Koolies Overseas Migration. Report of the Committee appointed by the Supreme Government of India to enquire into the abuses alleged to exist in exporting coolies and Indian labourers of various classes from Bengal Hill to other countries, together with an appendix containing the oral and written evidence taken by the committee and official documents laid before them, Calcutta, 1830.
2 Emigration Debate in British Parliament: Interview with J.H. Patton, magistrate of the 24 Pergunnahs, who was being examined regarding the method of enticing labourers.
3 Photo album of Mr Legene, KIT archive, Royal Tropical Institute, Amsterdam.
4 Tripathi (1923), *Kavita Kaumadi, teesra bhag*, Hindi Mandir: Sultanpur, Uttar Pradesh.
5 About the composition of the emigrant group to Suriname, De Klerk (1953) gives figures.
6 Examination of Mr Patton, the magistrate of 24 Pergunnahs, Bengal, in the report 'Emigration Debate in British Parliament', Report of the committee appointed

by the Supreme Government of India to enquire into the abuses alleged to exist in exporting coolies and Indian labourers of various classes from Bengal Hill to other countries, together with an appendix containing the oral and written evidence taken by the committee and official documents laid before them, Calcutta, 1940.

7  Examination of Ramdeen, Sardar and six coolies, men of Banaras, Seranpore and Gaya taken at the Townhall, on 10 December 1940. In Emigration Debate in British Parliament.

# 2

# *BIDESIA* AND SETTLEMENT HISTORIES IN SURINAME

With Maurits Hassankhan

*Sonwa karan aili ram, ehire marich des*
*Segati bhaile sonwa sarir, ehi re marich des*

(We came to this land because of money, and this money is the cause of the torture to our bodies).

(Bhikhari Thakur)
(Narayan 2005: 96)

## Arrival in Suriname and settlement

The story of the arrival of the migrants in Suriname and the conditions in which they lived there can be understood from the narrative of Baba Ambika Sarju, a hundred-year-old Bhojpuri migrant who was transported to Suriname in 1912. He belonged to Raebareli, and his father's name was Sarju. The name of the ship on which he, along with the other indentured labourers, travelled to Suriname was called *Matla Jahaj, Dui Lumber* (*Matla Ship No. 2*). According to historical records, this ship reached Suriname in 1912. Probing his memory, Ambika Sarju reported that almost 11,000 men travelled on the boat, but actual records show that only 310 men were on the boat. Ambika Sarju narrated in his own words how he landed in Suriname (Majumder 2010: 29, 31):[1]

> I was very young when my mother died. My father married again but my stepmother did not treat me well. I had to do all the household work like cutting grass, feeding the cattle and also cutting people's hair since I belonged to the barber caste. One day I heard my mother telling my aunt that she did not want to see my face again. That very day I decided to leave the village and earn my livelihood. I tied up my *chhura, kainchi, lota, thali, rajai* (knife, scissors, mug, plate and blanket), in a bundle and started for Bombay.

On the way I met a *halkati or arkatiya* (agent), who promised to take me to Bombay and get me a job there. But he made me get off at Kanpur and asked me to walk with a heavy load on my head thrice to see if I could carry the load. He then asked me if I would like to go with him for a job. At first I thought I would not go, but later I decided that it would be better if I went. Here I would only be a vagabond and end up in jail. Till then I did not know that the agent was planning to take me to Suriname. There was one *Sukulji* with me. I asked him whether he would accompany me to Suriname, which I first thought was quite close by (Majumder 2010: 31).

When we reached Suriname, we were given a five-year contract for working on the plantation. There were some Brahmins who came with us, but on seeing the nature of the work, they went back to India. The place where we worked was very miserable. We had to work from seven in the morning till four in the evening. On Saturdays we were let off at three. We had to cut grass, collect cow dung, sow cauliflower, *bakwa* (banana) and other vegetables. Mosquitoes and ants bit us all the time. In the evenings all the Bhojpuri migrants used to sit together and sing songs. There were people from many different communities among us. Back home, in each village there were different wells for the different castes but here there was no difference between the castes. The Brahmins also did not have any identification mark. About forty–fifty of us sat together around a well and sang songs of our *muluk* (country). But a few people who could not sing were asked to introduce themselves and talk about their native place. The good singers took the lead and we all followed (ibid).

Ambika Sarju went on to say that in spite of having a good house, good family and all comforts, he was deeply unhappy at having to leave his own country, his parents, his wife and other relatives. The loss was so tremendous that it could not be recovered. The only thing that helped him and the other migrants like him to express their sorrow was the folk song traditions in which they remembered their loss. Ambika Sarju sang a few lines from a folk song, which tells about the angst of the migrants (ibid):

*kalkatta se chhuta jahaj*
*hamra koi nahin*
*bhai bhi chhute, pita bhi chhute*
*bhaiya chhute abir*
*hamra koi nahin*
*hian Suriname aaye*

*kafri ke chal chaleye*
*kafri koi nahin*
  (Tiwari 2002)

*Translation*

The ship started from Calcutta,
but there was nobody with me.
My brother, father,
and also the colourful Holi festival
all got left behind.
Arrived here in Suriname,
followed the behaviour of creoles,
creoles are nothing.

Today Suriname is the smallest independent country on the South American continent with a multi-ethnic population comprising Creoles, Maroons, Javanese, Chinese, Hindustani indigenous people and others. The Hindustanis are the descendants of the Indian indentured labourers, and their language is called *Sarnami*. Today the Hindustanis form a large section of the population. In view of the fact that the maximum migration of indentured labourers to the Caribbean countries in the colonial period was from the rural regions of the Bhojpuri/Hindi-speaking belt of north-eastern India, the culture of all the Indo-Caribbean diasporic Indians was specifically the rural or peasant culture of that part of India. According to De Klerk (1953: 49) more than 92 per cent of the labourers came from western Bihar and eastern Uttar Pradesh. See figure 2.1. In contrast to the other labour-receiving countries, there were almost no migrants from South India. All ships departed from Calcutta, and the recruiting areas were mainly Bihar and Uttar Pradesh.

This is the reason that the Indians called themselves Hindustani: they came from Hindustan, where the lingua franca was Hindustani. They spoke and understood also Hindi/Urdu depending on their religious background. The culture of all the Indo-Caribbean diasporic Indians specifically reflects the rural or peasant culture of that part of India. From the different languages and dialects, they developed *Sarnami* Hindustani, which was a mixture of Bhojpuri, Awadhi and other local languages. The *Sarnami* Hindustani is now called *Sarnami*.

In 2004, the total number of Hindustanis in Suriname was 135,117, that is 27.4 per cent of the population, and the number of *Sarnami* speakers was 21,259 of the population (primary and secondary language

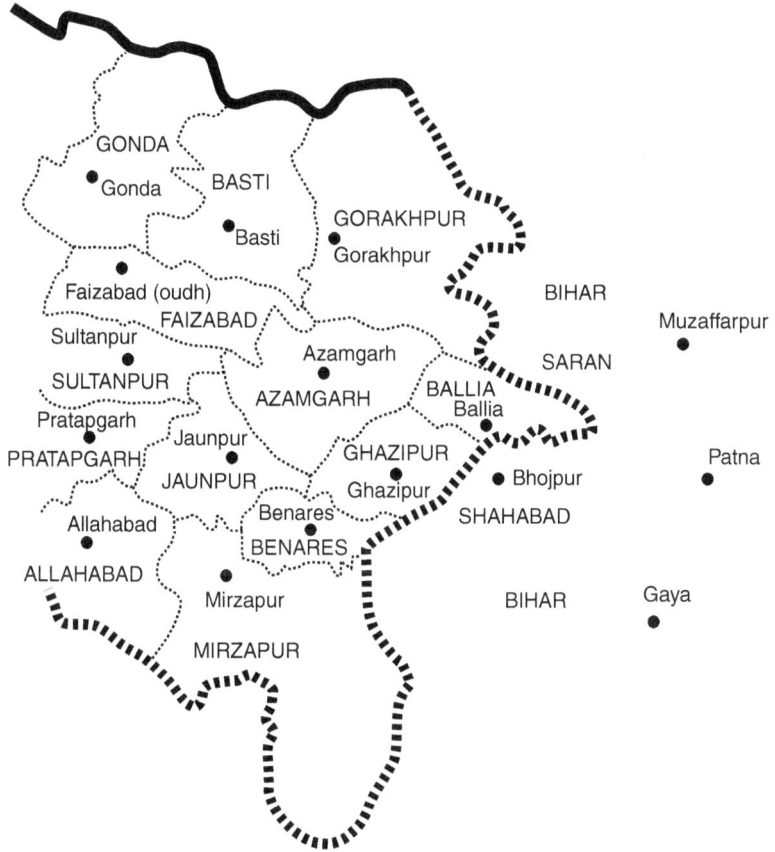

*Figure 2.1* Recruiting Areas for Suriname
Source: Based on De Klerk (1953: 47)

spoken in households). In 2012, the number of Hindustanis in Suriname was 148,443, that is 27.4 per cent of the population, and the number of *Sarnami* speakers was 534,541. The proportion of the Hindustani community speaking Hindustani in Suriname in 2004 was 82.9 per cent. One would be very pleased to observe that even after 130 years after the arrival of the *Lalla Rookh*, a proportion of 83 per cent of the Hindustanis used Hindustani as a means of communication within the family or household, whether as a primary language or secondary language. The matter of concern is, however, that the number of *Sarnami* speakers is decreasing.

In 2012 there were only 76.3 per cent of the Hindustanis who used Hindustani. This number decreased to 76.3 per cent, that is a decrease of 6.6 per cent within eight years. If we take the proportion of people who use *Sarnami* as primary language within the households, then there is more concern because these figures are 58.9 per cent for 2004 and 51.2 per cent for 2012. This is just above half of the Hindustani community.[2]

Suriname being one of the Caribbean countries to which the Bhojpuri labourers migrated, the Hindustani community of Suriname shares a similar culture with the Indo-Caribbeans in countries like Guyana and Trinidad or with Fiji, Mauritius, and the other countries where the Bhojpuri indentured labourers migrated. However, in spite of the inherent similarities with the other Indo-Caribbean diasporic Indians and also with the Bhojpuris living in India at present, the culture of the Hindustanis in Suriname is different from that of the Indo-Caribbeans in the other Caribbean countries because of the influence of the other ethnic cultures co-existing in Suriname. In this chapter, we will describe the historical processes of continuity and change that have taken place in the culture of the Hindustanis living in Suriname that is reflected in the culture of their present generations.

When the immigrants arrived in a totally different world in Suriname between 1873 and 1916, they struggled hard to rebuild their broken world, and in this process their collective memory and cultural heritage

*Figure 2.2* Group Portrait of Hindustani Indentured Labourers. Photograph: Julius Muller before 1895. Collection Surinaams Museum

*Figure 2.3* Hindustanis in Suriname, Wearing Traditional Costumes during Festivities in Front of the Government Palace at the Main Square in Paramaribo. Photograph: Augusta Curiel c. 1923. Collection Tropenmuseum 60006535

worked hand in hand in reshaping a new world that matched their own culture in all its diversity. Since the complete reconstruction of their old world was not possible, they continued with the means they had and re-created whatever of their culture, religion, music, festivals, arts, and so on, was allowed and possible. But at the same time they also adapted or adopted numerous elements from the other cultures present in the Caribbean. Thus the inherent Indianness has certainly been preserved to a great extent, but definitely not in its original form, because much has changed since the immigrants first arrived in Suriname in 1873. Suriname has a multi-ethnic society, with a large number of ethnic groups living in the country as a result of its colonization by Europeans from different countries who brought in people from various continents and ethnic, religious and cultural backgrounds to work on the sugarcane, cocoa, coffee and other plantations there. Originally, before it was colonized by the British and Dutch colonizers, the indigenous Amerindians populated the country. After the arrival of the Spaniards around 1500, there had been several efforts to colonize the region by French, British and Dutch. The first permanent European colonization took place by the British who possessed the colony until 1667, when the Dutch took over. Since 1664 there has been a colonization/settlement by Jews who came from the Portuguese colony of Brazil. These Portuguese Jews played an important role in the development of sugar cultivation in Suriname. In the initial colonization period, enslaved Africans were brought in to work on the plantations. After the abolition of slavery in 1863, Chinese, Hindustani and Javanese immigrants arrived in Suriname as substitutes for the former slave labour. During the time of slavery, many enslaved Africans fled into the woods and formed new communities. The ones who fled are known as Maroon, whereas those who stayed on the plantations and/or the city are known as Creoles. Both of these groups, that is the Maroon and the Creole, have their own distinct cultures. Moreover, the Guyanese and the Brazilians who immigrated into the country recently brought their cultures with them. The presence of so many different cultures in Suriname made it only natural for the Indian immigrants to integrate foreign elements into their culture. Their interactions with the other cultures due to the processes of immigration, acculturation, creolization, secularization, modernization and urbanization have resulted in the formation of a unique Indo-Surinamese culture that is not a simple 'transplant' or degraded version of that of the mother country, but is unique, having its own richness and depth (Manuel 2000: xiv). In other words, their culture differs not only from North Indian culture, but also from the cultures of most other diasporic groups (ibid: xiv).

Suriname consists also of Chinese and Javanese populations; both of these cultural groups were brought into Suriname as immigrants, respectively, since 1853 and since 1890. For studying the continuity and change that has taken place in the culture of the Indo-Caribbean diasporic Indians living in Suriname, the time period beginning from the initial migration of the Indo-Surinamese up to the present may be roughly divided into two cultural–historical phases. The first is the period of indentureship (1873–1921) characterized by deprivation, survival and violence, and the second is the post-indentureship period (1921–present) characterized by relative freedom and prosperity. The latter may be divided further into successive phases of (re-)construction (around 1921–1945) and modernization (around 1945–present).[3]

## Indentureship (1873–1921)

Relatively little is known about the cultural activities of indentured labourers during the earliest phase of indentureship, and to a lesser degree about their cultural way of life. Due to the hard-working and living conditions, their cultural life may be assumed to have practically been slowed down to a hibernating level. In other words, the first decades of indentured labour on the plantations were not so favourable for the enjoyment of social life, in general. This phase may, therefore, be characterized as the period of cultural survival and by aspects of survival such as opposition, revolt, confrontation, violence and resistance.

The exploitation of manual labour on the plantations left practically no time for leisure. The harsh working and living conditions and the economic desires of the planters and overseers often evoked violent and non-violent resistance in the plantations in other Caribbean countries. The situation in Suriname is reported to have been somewhat better because plantation owners allowed the indentured labourers 'a great amount of freedom after hours to preserve their own customs' (Ramsoedh and Bloemberg 1995: 13 f.). This means that they were given all facilities for meeting friends after working hours or during the weekend (McNeill 1915: 165) and that there was regular contact with compatriots on the neighbouring plantations (Speckmann 1965: 30). The planters also allowed some leisure to their labourers to celebrate certain festivals. Freedom of religion was guaranteed in the individual contracts and in the immigration convention between the Netherlands and the British government. According to this, the Muslim immigrants had sixteen recognized religious days, while the Hindus had thirty-two (De Klerk 1953: 131). Every year a calendar of the religious days was published by the government. On these days the immigrants could not be forced to work for their respective employers.

In fact the planters welcomed the festivals because they made more dangerous expressions of worker protest unnecessary or unlikely (Birbalsingh 1993: x; Mangru 1993: 17 ff.). Nevertheless, the workers appreciated the celebrations as an opportunity for relaxation, enjoyment and the unburdening of discontent. In this respect, some scholars like Ramsoedh and Speckmann appear to reflect the romantic view of colonial administrators or missionaries, namely that life on the plantation in Suriname was after all pleasant and worth enjoying. Other scholars like Hoefte (1998), Bhagwanbali (2010) and Hassankhan (2014) give another view of the plantation life, namely a life of suppression and exploitation. Maurits Hassankhan (2014: 225–226) states that the popular festival of *Muharram* or *Taziya* (*Tajiya*) can be seen as a form of protest. See figure 2.4. However, if the prevalent sense of cultural stagnation and survival and the persistent oral testimony of the Indo-Surinamese immigrants themselves are considered, the relative freedom and leisure enjoyed at the Surinamese plantations may be interpreted as mythical and elementary, obviously just sufficient for the Indic culture not to disintegrate and disappear, but to stay alive and survive.

*Figure 2.4* Hindustanis in Suriname with a *Tajiya*, c. 1890. Photograph: Julius Muller, before 1895. Collection Tropenmuseum 60005593

Ramsoedh and Bloemberg (1995) lists a number of factors that allowed East Indians in Suriname to preserve their customs, religion and culture relatively better than those in Guyana and Trinidad:

1. The attitude of the Dutch colonial authorities towards immigrants was not conducive to their fast absorption. As a result, the immigrants distinguished themselves from the rest of the society by their language and culture.
2. The regular supply of labourers provided an enduring bond with India.
3. Specific facilities for East Indians, such as education in their own language and the protection of the agent general and the British consul, strengthened cultural restoration.
4. The presence of members of the highest caste, the Brahmins (5 per cent), also contributed to this process. They managed to assume important positions as priests (pandits) in the restoration of certain customs and religious practices.
5. The prospect of returning to their mother country after five years did not stimulate the indentured labourers to adapt to their new situation culturally and linguistically.

6   Moreover, their relative isolation on the plantations and the corresponding labour specialization were not conducive to social and cultural assimilation. This isolation resulted in limited contacts with other groups of the population.
7   Furthermore, the immigrants were contracted for work that evoked the time of slavery, which dissociated the European–Creole society from the indentured labourers. These labourers did not fit into the cultural frame of reference of the Surinamese population. The East Indians for their part had a negative image of the Creoles (Speckmann 1965: 27 ff.; Ramsoedh and Bloemberg 1995: 13 f.). However, not all these aspects are unique for the Surinamese case. Others, also in the context of the *bidesia* project, stress that the main difference between Suriname and the British Caribbean is the difference in language. Suriname was a Dutch colony, and the Dutch were not inclined to impose the Dutch language on the immigrants, because they were supposed to stay temporarily in Suriname. They even introduced special schools for the immigrants on several plantations. After about 1900, the official policy changed: the so-called cooly schools were abolished and teaching took place officially in Dutch. However, in the rural areas there was a practice that in the lower classes of the basic school, the teachers used the native language of the local population. In the British Caribbean, the official language was English just as in British India. The immigrants learned English, and gradually the later generation lost their original language, while in Suriname the language was regarded as the key element of Indian culture and Indian identity. Another difference with the British Caribbean is the fact that in the British Caribbean many more Indians were baptized to Christianity. This was due to the influence of the Canadian Christian missionaries.[4]

In general, however, Indians were regarded with contempt by society at large in Suriname. Whites saw them as coolie heathens who drank excessively, abused their wives, dressed like savages and clung to their backward ways and pagan faiths (Manuel 2000: 4). Indian marriages were not legally recognized until 1940, and all Indian children were illegitimate in the eyes of the state. Facing such hostility and limited employment opportunities, the Hindustani migrants tended to remain on rural farms and plantations, leaving the towns and cities to Creoles, who enjoyed a head start in education and language and who largely shunned plantation labour. Gradually, however, the Hindustanis rapidly progressed socially, which caused a number of the existing prejudice against this group to disappear. On the other hand, it gave rise to new problems, as the Creoles were beginning to fear that the Hindustanis would economically outstrip them, and they sometimes expressed this fear in aggressive behaviour. Some Hindustanis also started displaying the beginning of a feeling of superiority in respect of the other groups, partly as a reaction to the attitude of the majority of the Creoles, partly as a result of the self-confidence of a newly developing group.

In this respect, we can mention the founding of associations of immigrants around 1910, the *Surinaamse Immigranten Vereniging* (Surinamese Immigrants Association, SIV) and the *Ekhtiar aur Hak* (rights and share). They tried to unite the immigrants and to promote the interests of the Indian immigrants. They protested against the use of the word *koelie* for the Indians, and they called themselves Hindustanis.

Since 1895 the government of Suriname induced the settlement of Indian immigrants in Suriname. They could get a piece of land, and those who abandoned their right on free return passage received an amount of money, which they could use to start as small farmer or peasant. Many Indians used this opportunity and settled as small farmers in different rural districts. Their main product was rice, while all small farmers had also some cows, chicken, ducks, goats and so on. They also produced their own vegetables.

## Post-indentureship (1921–present)

After the termination of the recruitment of indentured labourers in India in 1918, it was clear that most of the time-expired labourers would stay in their respective countries of destination. Many migrants were successful in starting a new life. They were also aware of the fact that many migrants who went back to India decided to migrate a second time, whether to the same colony or another. Since the arrival of the last emigrant ship in Suriname in 1916 but more since 1921, the ties with the motherland seemed to be cut of. There were no new arrivals, and the return of migrants to India was sporadic, because there were no retourships available. Those who wanted to return could only do it via Demerara (De Klerk 1953; Choenni and Choenni 2012: 30).

After a phase of cultural deprivation and stagnation during indentureship, there followed a period of relative freedom and prosperity for the Hindustanis in which there was ample opportunity for cultural expression. The Asian communities also gradually began claiming their place in the urban life of Paramaribo although during the initial decennia of their arrival they had lived in the districts. In addition to their hard work and reverence for land of the Indians, in general, World War I played an important role in improving the living conditions of the immigrants. All this stimulated further organized cultural celebrations. They also started forming a number of Hindustani organizations including the SIV, replaced by *Nawa Yuga Oeday* (rise of a new era), which was founded in 1924. From the 1930s onwards numerous important Hindustani institutions came up, such as religious organizations, temples, mosques, schools, orphanages and radio stations. Notable is the influence of radio, TV and especially Bollywood cinema and music in shaping the further course of the culture of the Hindustanis of Suriname until the present. World War II played an important role in the development of Surinamese society, including the Indian community. During the war there was an accelerated process of urbanization, which also affected the Hindustani community. Hindustanis learned to value education and started to send their children to schools in large numbers. Educated people left agriculture and sought employment in other sectors. Many people from the outer districts moved to or in the vicinity of Paramaribo, because all major facilities and services were available only there. As a consequence of this, majority of the people are living in Greater Paramaribo. This had its impact also on social, economic and cultural aspects of their life.

After World War II the Hindustanis also became politically active and integrated in the Surinamese society and evolved gradually as equal citizens of the country.

After a long period of time, the cultural baggage could be opened again, and ancient Indian rites and traditions, such as marriage and funeral rites, were reanimated. There was both the reconstruction of older forms such as family life and the construction of newer forms, for example their language (*Sarnami*), music (*baithak-gana*) and many other customs and habits, which emerged in fresh and innovative forms in this period.

### (Re-)construction (about 1921–1945)

After serving their contract on the estates, most of the immigrants decided to stay in Suriname temporarily or permanently. About one-third of the migrants eventually returned to India, while about 17 per cent of them did not survive their indenture. As a consequence not two-thirds, but about 50 per cent, of the migrants settled in Suriname.[5] About 50 per cent of those who arrived in Suriname or 60 per cent of those who survived indenture opted for staying in Suriname, and they were usually rewarded by a piece of land and some cash (i.e. 100 Dutch guilders).[6] On their land they worked hard and soon prospered with the income they generated by selling their crops. They profited especially during and after World War I. The post–World War I period brought prosperity and development for most of the East Indians of Suriname. Due to the war, the import of food stagnated in the colonies, and it is this opportunity that was seized by the Indo-Caribbeans to change their economic destiny. Towards the end of indentureship, many Hindustanis had already acquired land and settled as small farmers. They constituted the small farming sector, which was put up and stimulated by the local government to serve as a buffer for plantation farming (Ramsoedh and Bloemberg 1995: 9). This sector proved its value during the food shortages caused by the war as it turned out to be the very backbone of the Surinamese economy. Towards the end of the 1930s, the total production capacity of small farming exceeded that of plantation farming (ibid). The economic success of the small farming sector ultimately led to the improvement in the living standards of the Hindustanis. One may thus infer from this situation that it was only after World War I that Indo-Caribbean culture, religion, music, drama, and so on could be expressed and enjoyed more leisurely than before.

From the 1930s onwards, many important Hindustani institutions came up, such as the recognition of the *adat* (customary law) in marital affairs and the construction of temples, mosques, orphanages, cemeteries and so on. These factors provided time and space for Hindustanis to enjoy

*Figure 2.5* Hindustanis Wearing Ram Lila Costumes at a Performance on a Location between Paramaribo and Uitkijk, in Suriname. Photograph: C. van der Koppel c. 1930–1940. Collection Tropenmuseum 10019302

*Figure 2.6* Portrait of a Hindustani Woman in Suriname. Photographer Unknown, between 1900 and 1920. Collection Tropenmuseum 10019396 and 60006494

their culture and customs *more* elaborately and leisurely. In other words, as soon as indentured labour was over and Hindustanis worked on their own ground and for their own prosperity, they thrived and could spend more time and money on their cultural needs. It is this spirit of freedom and entrepreneurship that triggered, on the one hand, the revival of rites, customs, feasts and festivals, and, on the other, the formation of the first *samáj-s*, social and cultural organizations, such as music bands and drama or Ram Lila troupes, which performed at religious and cultural events – immediately after indentureship. See figure 2.5.

In the period after termination of their indenture, the Hindustanis, most of whom were (young) individuals, reconstructed their family life. The most common was the joint family, which existed until the 1970s and 1980s. In the 1920s and 1930s there were also panchayats in the rural areas. The Hindustanis had their own *mandirs* (temples) and masjids, with, respectively, a Hindi and an Urdu school, where religious education was given. Around 1930, countrywide religious umbrella organizations were founded, namely *Shri Sanátan Dharm Mahá Sabhá*, the *Arya Dewaker* and the *Surinaamse Islamitische Vereniging* (*Surinamese Islamic Association* – SIV), while in 1931 the *Khiláfat Anjuman* was founded. Through Trinidad and Guyana, religious reformers reached Suriname and contributed to the cultural reorientation of the Indian heritage: the *Ahmadiyas* soon dominated the Sunnis of the *Surinaamse Islamitische Vereniging*. The *Ahmadiya* movement in Suriname was known as a modern reform movement within Islam and was quite popular. The *Arya Samaj* (noble society) found its platform when in 1930 the *Arya Dewaker* was founded. On 31 July 1929 an *Arya Samaj* clergyman, Jaimini Mehta Ji, spoke in Loge Concordia on Indian culture and theosophy (Van Kempen IV: 16). The founder of the *Arya Samaj*, Dayanand Saraswati (1824–1883), propagated ideas which very much appealed to the immigrants. He had started a war on the social abuse in the East Indian society and the caste system and propagated a better position for women. Moreover, he advocated the right to travel (overseas) to search for their welfare elsewhere in the world, a right that he defended in his most important work the *Satyartha Prakash* (light of true meaning) with reference to the *Mahabharata*.

## Modernization (1945–1975)

During and after World War II there was a political awakening of the Hindustanis. Until then they were politically non-active, but since 1943 there was a broad movement in Suriname for political autonomy. The Hindustanis generally had been treated as foreigners, and they wanted to become full citizens. In 1943 came the *Vereniging Djágaran* (awakening), and in 1946 the *Liga van Hindustani's* (Hindustani Liga). Also within the Hindustani group differentiation increased steadily. After the war several political parties were founded, that is the Muslim Party, the Hindu Party and the Hindustani–Javanese Political Party. In 1949 the *Verenigde Hindostaanse Party* (United Hindustani Party) was founded in order to unite the Hindustanis and to work on their economic, socio-cultural and political emancipation.

The fast-increasing number of Hindustani socio-cultural organizations had their own accommodations for cultural manifestations. In this way, *Shánti Dal*, which existed since 1948, started using her own *Sanskriti Bhavan* in the Annie Street, where many pieces were performed. In 1968 *Mátá Gauri* was opened in Kwatta (Van Kempen IV: 285). In 1949 the first general elections on the basis of universal suffrage took place. Since then the Hindustanis were represented in parliament, and later they participated in the government. The political emancipation since the introduction of universal suffrage and the foundation of political parties after World War II contributed considerably to their emancipation in other fields.

The most influential factor that changed the life and culture of the Indo-Caribbeans, next to the elevating effects of World War I, came with the arrival of mass media such as radio, cinema and later television in the Caribbean. 'The arrival of the first sound films, along with the Indian records, starting with *Bálá Joban* in 1935, played a crucial role in igniting a cultural revival among the East Indian community of Trinidad' (Manuel 2000: 44; Gooptar 2014). This also applies for Suriname because local distributors of Indian films and records also imported the same material in 1936. Until then the life and culture on the plantation of the Indo-Caribbeans and later on the small farms had hardly changed, as they were caught in a fixture of conservatism and traditionalism.

The AVROS (*Algemene Vereniging Radio Omroep Suriname*), the first radio station in Suriname, came on the air in 1935. During the war school headmaster J.P. Kaulesar Sukul began with weekly broadcasts of Hindustani music.

Until 1957 this was the only broadcasting station in Suriname (Van Kempen IV: 44). The new and fresh melodies and beats of Hindi film music, broadcasted from the newly established radio stations, could not remain without affecting the minds of the Indo-Caribbeans. Indian cultural workers hired broadcasting time on radio stations and were very popular. These programmes were also used for death announcements and for *khás farmáis* for movie songs at the occasion of weddings, birthdays and departure of relatives to the Netherlands (*Bidesia Sourcebook Suriname*). Notable effects were the imitation of dialogues, fashion and coiffure of favourite actors. A new phase developed with the establishment of the first Hindustani radio station Radika in 1962. Presently there are a number of Indian radio- and television stations, bringing in the living room of all homes Bollywood movies, serials and so on.

It should be noted that Hindustani culture in Suriname could not have been maintained without Bollywood films and their omnipresent music. From 1936 the cinemas began screening East Indian movies such as *Fashionable India* on the life in Bombay depicted in dance, music and songs (Van Kempen IV: 40). Hindi films have been very popular right from their introduction till the present day.

Though often highly theatrical and romanticized, these movies provided, in a way, a direct or visual contact with homeland India. Especially pictures depicting rural life, such as *Mother India, Ganga–Jamuna*, and *Jis Desh men Ganga Bahti hai*, have been extremely popular. The high values depicted in religious or historical movies such as *Mahabharata, Ramáyana* and *Raja Harishchandra* certainly must have had an edifying effect on their viewers.

The Hindi language spoken in these movies not only has helped the people to keep their knowledge of the language alive but also appears to have functioned as a rich substrate for the vocabulary of *Sarnami*. In this regard the positive role of the numerous cinema halls and radio stations should not be underestimated. Bollywood music, for example, has had an everlasting influence on the further development of the local music of the Indo-Surinamese people.

*Baithak-gana*, a musical form that originated on Surinamese soil around 1920, became a popular means for public entertainment in the following decades. This music reached its first zenith in the 1950s and once again in the 1980s. Between 1971 and 1975, some important national and international *baithak-gana* contests were held in Paramaribo. Even though such contests were now and then organized till the end of the second millennium, the heydays of *baithak-gana* were between 1971 and 1975.

## Independence and the second wave of diaspora (1975–present)

Suriname received development from the Netherlands since 1948, and this contributed to create a certain degree of welfare in the country. The cultural policy was based on tolerance and respect for all cultures and religions within the multi-cultural society. Since the 1960s, there was an increase of outmigration to the Netherlands, because for many people the Dutch welfare society, and not other Third World countries, was a reference point for their aspirations. For most of them, the travel cost to the Netherlands was too high, the reason that migration was on relatively small scale.

Since the 1960s there was also a nationalist movement that aimed for the independence of the country. The Hindustani political parties were of the opinion that economic independence should precede the political independence of the country. They advocated a gradual way to independence. When a new elected government announced in 1974 that the country would become independent not later than the end of 1975, many people were uncertain about the future of the country. There were for the first time communal tensions in Suriname. The country became divided, and many people began to sell their properties and tried to leave the country. A large section of the Hindustani community, which had not supported independence, chose to migrate to the Netherlands. Those who could not leave felt insecure. Diasporic dynamics were once again activated, and people started moving towards other countries such as the United States, Canada and other neighbouring countries. The largest groups of Surinamese, however, went to the Netherlands. There, the relatively traditional Hindustani community, some generations after the first migration, was once again confronted with a new environment, lifestyle, cuisine and so on. The cultural shock may, to a certain degree, be compared to the situation when the first Indian indentured labourers arrived in the Caribbean and faced the alien and hostile cultures of whites and blacks. The main difference now was that they went 'voluntarily' there and were not taken by surprise, as they already knew what to expect in Europe, and, most important, the Dutch were not hostile this time. Moreover, the modern means of communications and transportation softened the pains of separation considerably. It did not take long for the different communities to adjust themselves to the new situation and take up their daily life. The Hindustanis quickly organised their community and set up numerous religious and cultural organizations and societies, which provided them full opportunity to express and nurture their cultural and musical heritage. See figure 2.7.

In Suriname, on the other hand, as a result of almost half of the Indian population migrating, the internal cohesion of the country suffered. This became particularly visible in the economy of Suriname, whereas in the 1980s and 1990s, the country was reeling under military rule, which also targeted radio stations, and by economic hardships. In cultural respect,

*Figure 2.7* Sarees and Bangles in a Hindustani Supermarket in Rotterdam. Photograph: Sarojini Lewis, 2006

musicians began experimenting with Western and Caribbean rhythms and melodies. Certain trends, for example, *Chutney* music, which had already set in in the 1960s, became extremely popular in the final three decades of the second millennium. The role of *Sarnami* language in society also underwent a change. The language was now spoken and explored by writers both in Suriname and in the Netherlands, whereas *Sarnami* also was used now by religious officials and politicians during events like election campaigns alongside the prestige languages like Hindi, Urdu, English and Dutch. On the other hand, more and more people used Dutch as a language spoken at home, instead of or alongside *Sarnami*. Next to Dutch, Hindustanis also are using Sranan Tongo as common language in the public sphere. The *Sarnami* gradually converted into an in-group language of the Hindustani ethnic group. It was hardly ever used in education (Damsteegt 2002: 252). During the 1980s the government decided to recognize Surinamese languages and to standardize the spelling of all Surinamese languages, including *Sarnami*. As a consequence there is an official Roman spelling of *Sarnami*.

After the short period of cultural hiatus in the 1970s and the early 1980s, it is heartening to see that the Hindustanis have once again started expanding their social and cultural life. Their function in Suriname now comprises of a complex amalgam of strengthening their own group position, increasing the social input of the group and contributing to Surinamese nation building. The following is one example of practical adjustment to the new situation. Since the military coup of February 1980, there was a curfew, as a consequence of which people could not go out of their homes at night. This meant, among others, a blow to all cinemas. Watching movies in cinemas was replaced by watching them through DVDs. DVD rental shops experienced a boom, while cinemas closed one after the other. A new development was the establishment of television stations and radio stations owned by Indians. These stations broadcasted Indian/Hindustani programmes. Most Bollywood movies and Hindi serials are broadcasted, and the people can watch them free of charge. Through this, there is a certain degree of promotion of Indian languages such as Hindi, Urdu and *Sarnami*. Popular interactive programmes in Dutch and *Sarnami* contribute to the preservation of the Indian culture. Through Bollywood films, the Hindustanis in Suriname also discover other aspects of the Indian culture like the Hindu traditions, which were not known or were not practised in Suriname before.

The status of *Sarnami* is once again reviving, and with the publication of his poetry in *Sarnami*, Jit Narain, a famous poet of Suriname, has placed that language with a bang on the map for all to hear, thereby giving notice of its presence and taking its rightful place among the other national languages of the land. In the field of music, one may discern a post-modern *baithak-gana* period because both in Suriname and in the Netherlands there are numerous musicians, who besides singing *chutney* and other modern genres revert to the classical *baithak-gana*.

Thus the rather turbulent history of the Indo-Caribbean people in Suriname shows that they have gone through numerous ups and downs, but every time their culture survived, apparently because of its suppleness and resiliency. The Hindustanis are now more and more becoming global citizens since a large number of Surinamese Hindustanis are also migrating to countries like the United States, Canada and other neighbouring countries, apart from the Netherlands, but they are making arduous efforts to keep ties with their homeland. These groups of immigrants and also their children feel themselves as children of Suriname, without, however, giving up their love, respect and loyalty to India.

Many Hindustanis from Suriname and the Netherlands are traveling to India, combining vacation with shopping and search for roots. According to informal conversations with those who have visited India, they express their gratitude to their ancestors who under difficult circumstances left their home and started a new life in Suriname. On the other hand, there are also Hindustanis who are shocked when they visit India. Although they know that India is now a big and fast-developing country, they are shocked by the poverty of people sleeping on footpaths or in shabby homes just in the vicinity of their hotels.

## Notes

1 Ambika, son of Sarjoo, arrived in Suriname at the age of eighteen on Ship *Mutlah III*, 13 June 1913. His contract was on plantation Peperpot, at the right bank of Suriname River. Place of origin: District: Raebareli. Thana: Sareni. Village: Bhoopsinghkapurwa. The *Mutlah III* arrived with 645 immigrants. Contr Nr PP/1–645. His own ID Nr was PP/559. He belonged to the cast of *nau(barber)*. Source: Maurits Hassankhan and Sandew Hira, *Historical Database Suriname. The data on the Indian Immigrants*, vol. 3, p. 727. Paramaribo/The Hague, IMWO/Amrit, 1998.

2 ABS (General Bureau for Statistics), Census Reports 2004: vol 4, p. 32; 2012, vol. 3, p. 53.

3 The first period ends in 1921 when the contract of the last immigrants expired. The phase of reconstruction ended between 1940 and 1945 (World War II). World War II changed the Surinamese society in almost all aspects. It marks also the end of the plantation period and the beginning of a new era, with other economic sectors becoming more important, political awareness of immigrant groups, the introduction of parliamentary system and socio-cultural changes. The phase of 1945–present can be divided in to 1945–1975 (the year of independence) and 1975–present. The year of 1975 is important because of the mass migration of people, which caused socio-economic and cultural changes and problems.

4 Against this argument, it can be stated that in Fiji, also a British colony, the language of the immigrants survived just as in Suriname. The only reason could be that Suriname and Fiji are countries where indentured immigration started very late (1873 and 1879, respectively), while in the Anglophone Caribbean Indian immigration began in 1838/1845.
5 In almost all works it is mentioned that about one-third went back to India, while two-thirds settled in the colony. It is the merit of Bhagwanbali (2010: 135) that he counted the numbers of indentured labourers who did not survive their indenture (National Archives Suriname (NAS), Immigration Department, data on arrivals and repatriation of immigrants). This number was 16 per cent. This means that actually only 50 per cent of the labourers settled permanently in Suriname.
6 According to the figures given by Bhagwanbali, 5,490 labourers died during indenture. The number of survivors was therefore 28,721. The number of repatriates was 11,663, that is 40 per cent of the survivors. This conclusion is based on the figures of the immigration department in the NAS.

# 3

# DOUBLE MIGRATION AND SILENCED HISTORY

## Hindustanis from Suriname to the Netherlands

*Nehwa Lagake Dukhwa De Gaile Re Pardesi Saiyyan*
*Apne Ta Gaile Paapi, Likhiyo Na Bheje Paati*
(Mahendra Mishra)
(Singh 1958: 217)

*(You showered your love and affection then broke my heart migrating to a distant land*
*You yourself went away and did not even send a letter)*

### Settlement in the Netherlands

Since the end of the 1960s, but especially around 1975, when Suriname attained independence from the Netherlands, many of the Bhojpuris who had stayed behind in Suriname after the expiration of their contract period left for the Netherlands. This second migration was because of political trouble and uncertainty about the development of society after independence. The fear of Creole domination, exaggerated by the politicians, created a fear of a 'Guyanese situation', and many Hindustanis decided to move to Holland overnight (Majumder 2010: 33). All that had been built up with great effort in Suriname was given up, namely land, property, trees and the consecrated corner with the holy bamboo flags and tulsi plants. All the fields that the grandparents had wrested from the jungle had to be abandoned. Most of the people who moved to Holland considered the move to be a temporary one lasting a few years – five years at the very most. However, almost all the younger generations who moved to Holland continued to stay on there.

At present some 160,000 Hindustanis live in the Netherlands. About 40,000 Hindustanis live in The Hague and its suburbs, while the rest

*Figure 3.1* Group Portrait of Women and Children, Hindustani Indentured Labourers. Photograph: Julius Muller before 1895. Collection Tropenmuseum 60008925

are scattered in cities such as Amsterdam, Rotterdam and Utrecht, and elsewhere all over the country. Interestingly, just like the Hindustanis living in Suriname had consciously preserved their cultural heritage in order to retain their Bhojpuri Indian identities, the Hindustanis who migrated to Holland also maintain their own religion, cultural habits and celebrations while living in Dutch society. This attempt can be seen by the presence of several *mandirs* as well as shops with tropical vegetables, which can be found everywhere. The Hindustanis also attempt to grow all kinds of Indian vegetables like *keraila* (bitter gourd), *bora* (beans), *mirca* (green chilli) and *sag* (green leafy vegetables) in glasshouses in their own yards. Many of these attempts prove to be successful. In general the Dutch Hindustanis have made themselves at home in the Netherlands by integrating into the Dutch culture while maintaining their basics, which have an age-old origin (ibid: 33, 35). They project an image of an enterprising, hard-working, thrifty group that has smoothly integrated in Dutch society.

## Indianization

The Indian culture, which had been passed down from father to son and from mother to daughter over generations after migration to Suriname, has continued to be passed down in Holland. Initially, when the Hindustanis first arrived in the Netherlands, they were awed by the material affluence, luxury and comfort in Holland and tried to pursue the same thing. There was a hunger for comfort, a washing machine, a refrigerator, a car in front of the door, a house of their own and a holiday once a year. However, despite the material comforts the Hindustanis in the Netherlands tried to cling on to their cultural inheritance. The same clothing, diet and etiquettes and pictures of gods and goddesses that had been stuck on the walls of their houses in Suriname continued to be followed (Majumder 2010: 101). See figure 3.2.

For Hindustani women, migration to the Netherlands was a big step forward as they could afford the luxury of various modern conveniences that they did not have access to in Suriname. As a result, their lives got a lot easier and over the years the social position of Hindustani women has improved considerably. In addition to this, the position of women in relation to that of men in Dutch society is much better than in Suriname. In the Netherlands, it is, in the most case, the woman who can expel the

*Figure 3.2* Hindu Gods in the House of a Hindustani Migrant from Suriname in the Netherlands. Photograph: Sarojini Lewis, 2006

man from the house than vice versa. However, parallel to the pursuit of a relative prosperity, the Surinamese Hindustanis in Holland have a constant need to assert and exhibit their own culture. In Suriname they were never asked where they came from. Neither was there any interest in each other's cultural tradition and practices. Everyone did his or her thing and accepted the curious customs of the other. In the Netherlands, however, Hindustanis have to redefine themselves whether they are Dutch, Surinamese, Hindustani Surinamese or Indian. Some people are aware of their multiple identities, which depend on specific circumstances. The older-generation Hindustanis have the ties with Suriname, with their cultural orientation also to India. The newer generations tend to look more to India than the older generation. In addition to that, an air ticket to Suriname is more expensive than one to India (ibid: 102).

In some cases Hindustanis from Suriname living in the Netherlands feel tempted to say that they are from India, thereby implying that they belong to a rich cultural tradition. Telling a vague story about Bihar and Uttar Pradesh and that their ancestors went to Suriname as coolies instead of claiming that their ancestors came straight from the *Taj Mahal* makes them feel inferior. Accordingly, Surinamese Hindustanis prefer to claim that they belong to a rich culture even though they hardly know anything about Indian culture. After all, everything from India is considered holy. In reality, most Hindustanis do not know more about India beyond what they have picked up here and there. In Holland there are several stores with clothes and goods from India that sell books on yoga, a translation of the *Bhagavad Gita* or the *Upanishad*. This ambiguity of wanting to be as Indian as possible, while obsessively holding on to what one originally took with him or her as well as turning away from Dutch culture, led to isolation and a generation gap among a certain set of people. However, at present Dutch Hindustanis are trying hard to learn the nuances of Indian culture, and classical dance from India is very popular among Hindustani girls (ibid: 103).

Their language, *Sarnami*, however, seems to be under threat since the second and third generation of the Hindustani immigrants hardly use this language. In the Netherlands, a perfect command of the Dutch language is required. With the loss of *Sarnami* as one's mother tongue, one loses more than memories of parents and grandparents. A direct connection with one's own origin ceases to exist. Identity has everything to do with memory, and memory is connected with language. Today many Hindustanis in Holland like to claim Hindi as their mother tongue. Bombay fashion can be found all around due to the influence of Bollywood films. Another way by which Dutch Hindustanis remain connected with India is by frequently travelling to India. They visit holy places like Haridwar and Varanasi, and practically all of them have a vague idea about visiting their ancestral village. However, only very few have been successful in tracing back their village. Today the Hindustanis in the Netherlands have forayed into almost all professions and are making their mark in each of them. The Hindustani community has now attained a good level of affluence, but alongside there is an increasing urge to remain connected with their roots.

# 4

# *BIDESIA* FOLK CULTURE IN THE TRIANGLE

## Bhojpuri region of India, Suriname and the Netherlands

### With Narinder Mohkamsingh

*Piya Tajke Hame Gaile Pardeswa Na*
*Gaye Hamse Karke Ghaat, Sun Sautin Ke saath*
*Naahi Bhejal Jabse Gaile Sandeswa Na*
(Rupan)
(Singh 1958: 199)

*(My husband left me and went to a distant land*
*He ditched me and went, he is now with other woman*
*He has not even sent a word from the time he left)*

## *Bidesia* folk culture in India

The mass migration from the Bhojpuri region was a heavy emotional loss both for the people who were left behind and for the people who were leaving. Before they realized, many tender relationships were torn apart: wives from their husbands, sisters from her brothers, a father's old-age support who was an apple of his mother's eye. All were leaving for foreign shores, and there was no way to hold them back. The labourers who were migrating under this system too had little hopes of returning. They were going away to a far-off land from where it was difficult to communicate. Some migrants did return, but instead of going back to their native place, they usually stayed back in Calcutta, taking up some small jobs to earn their living. So for the Bhojpuri society, this pain was very deep. That is why these migrants were addressed as *bidesia*, that is those who have become foreigners. The pain arising from this separation gave birth to a distinct folk culture that was called *bidesia* folk culture. It was a holistic folk culture that included songs, poetry, drama, dance, art and so on, narrating the anguish of both the people who were left behind and those who were leaving for foreign shores. Since very little folk tradition is written and published, it is difficult to fix the exact time period when this folk culture emerged, but the word *bidesia* in Bhojpuri folk culture started being used around the same time as when the overseas migration to the Caribbean countries began. In the Bhojpuri folk culture, the concept of *pardes* (a place away from the home) is slightly different from the concept of *bides* (foreign). The word *bides* incorporates the idea of distance and of becoming strangers. In 1858, a prostitute named Sundari living in Banaras used the word *bides* as a form of address in her compositions. In 1884 Pandit Beni Ram, a resident of Kashi, composed a folk song in which the word *bidesia* was used for the first time to address a person who has left and gone away (Majumder 2010: 144–145).

*Kahe mori sudhi bisaraye re bidesia*
*Tarhpi tarhpi din raina gavayo re*
*Kahe mose nehiya lagae re bidesia.*
 (Pandit Beni Ram)
 (Singh 1958: 142)

*Translation*

Why did you make me lose my consciousness, O *bidesia*?
I am suffering constantly day and night.
Why did you lock your eyes with mine, O *bidesia*?

Composition of *bidesia* folk songs also started from this point of time, which later formed the base for the *bidesia* folk culture. In these songs for the first time, the word *bidesia* is used as a 'tek'. Scholars believe that this is the special and unique feature of *bidesia* folk tradition (Majumder 2010: 145).

*Gawna karaye saiyan ghar baithvale se*
*Apne lobhile pardes re bidesia*
*Charhli jawania bairin bhaili hamri se*
*Ke mora harihen kales re bidesia*
*Bhabki ke chadli main apni atariya se*
*Charu ore chitwon chihai re bidesia*
*Katahu na dekho rama saiyan ke suratiya se*
*Jiyara gaile murajhai re bidesia*
 (Bhikhari Thakur)
 (Singh 1958: 221)

*Translation*

You made me sit at home after marriage, but you yourself went away, O *bidesia*.
My youth is my own enemy.
There is no one to fulfil me, O *bidesia*.
I am sitting on the terrace of my house, eagerly awaiting your arrival, O *bidesia*.
I cannot see my beloved anywhere, and my flower-like heart is slowly withering away, O *bidesia*.

In 1906, a composition called *Sundari Vilap*, which was composed by Sri Ram Sakal Pathak Dwijram in 1896, was published. Sri Ram Sakal Pathak was a resident of Sahanipatti, in the Buxar district. The *bidesia* folk music tradition developed because of this composition, which is popular even today. This music was further developed by Pandit Beni Ram. Before 1886, the pain caused by the process of migration was only fleetingly mentioned, but after this composition, the pain that resulted from the separation came to be described vividly. The anguish, which emerged from the description of the migrants, became the second significant feature of the *bidesia* folk tradition. The songs of *Sundari Vilap*, which were composed by Dwijram, describe the phenomenon of *bidesia* in the following manner (Majumder 2010: 145–146). The following two lines depict the expressions of the beauty of the migrant husband.

*Othwa ta haue ram kataral panwa se*
*Nakwa suganwa Ke thor se bidesia*
        (Dwivedi 2000: 38)

*Translation*

You have thin lips like a betel leaf that has been cut in half.
Your nose is like the beak of a parrot, O *bidesia*.

The tune to which this song was set came to be used as the main tune of the *bidesia* folk songs. 'Sundari', who has been deserted by her beloved, describes her sorrow in the song (Majumder 2010: 146).

In 1910, a composition was edited by Shri Nath Sharan, called *Pyari Sundari Viyog (bidesia)*, which had twenty parts. This was published in 1912 by Kausadhan Pustakalaya, Nakhas Chowk, Gorakhpur. This was also a collection of compositions of various folk composers.

On the level of form, rhythm and metre, *bidesia* folk tradition has three characteristics.

1. There are two lines in the 'bund'.
2. The first line ends with the 'tek' and 'se', while the second line ends with the word *bidesia*.
3. There are heart-rending and sorrowful tunes with a high-pitched alap (ibid).

The tunes are usually in the form of wailing. Even today when brides leave for the house of their in-laws after marriage, they can be heard crying on this tune since *bidesia* songs were the outcome of sadness caused by separation. On the level of metre (*chhand*), Bhikhari Thakur, the most popular exponent of *bidesia* folk culture in the Bhojpuri region, adopted the features mentioned earlier. In addition he introduced 'teks' like *balmua* and *piyawa*(husband). In other metres also, he has talked about migration (ibid).

*Piyawa gailan kalkattva e sajani*
*Turi dihlan pati-patni natawa e sajni*
(ibid: 39)

*Translation*

Your husband has gone to Calcutta, O *sajani*,
breaking the ties of husband and wife.

*Bitat baate ath pahariya ho dahariya johat na*
*Dhoti patdhariya dhaike kanhwa par chadariya ho*
*Babariya jhaari ke na*
*Hoiba kavna sahariya ho babariya jhaari ke na*
(Bhikhari Thakur)
(Yadav and Singh (ed.) 2005: 25)

*Translation*

I am spending all my time waiting for my beloved.
To which land have you gone, wearing your dhoti and *gamchha*.
God knows where you are now, with your hair properly combed.

The following folk song sung by female agricultural labourers of the Bhojpuri regions during the season of the paddy crops connotes the social, cultural and emotional loss of the family, relatives and Bhojpuri folk (Majumder 2010: 147).

> *Railiya na bairi se jahajawa na bairi se paisawa bairi na*
> *mor saiyan ke bilmawe se paiswa bairi na*
> (Narayan 2005: 70)

*Translation*

> It is neither the train nor the ship that is our enemy
> but rather the money that compels our husband to migrate to other lands.

These lines carry the angst of a separated married womenfolk (Priya, beloved) who understand that the separation is caused by the need to earn a living at a place that is far away (ibid).

In the following Bhojpuri folk song, a woman sadly sings:

> The arhar rots in the field of arhar
> In the pitcher rots the flour
> The wife rots in the mother's house
> The husband rots in Bides
> (Narayan 2005: 73)

Even when a husband returns, he has no strength left in his body. One folk song describes the state of the migrant after returning to his native land:

> After twelve years my husband returned
> My husband returned after wasting his life
> He came with grown hair
> (Narayan 2005: 73)

The wives of the migrants have to suffer many hardships because when the husbands stay away for a long time and do not send home enough money, they are likely to be ill-treated and even necessities of life may be grudged. Normally as the joint family system prevails, a woman expects support from the brothers of her husband and other members of the family. But the prolonged absence of men puts too much strain on the system. Here are a few lines from a touching *jantsar* (grinding mill) song:

> I cooked puris for everybody and *the juar for the children*
> but that food became poison
> as the prince went away to a foreign land (bides).

My mother-in-law asked me 'on whose earnings will you live?'
My mother-in-law's offspring is Lakhan devar; I shall live upon his earnings.
'I have a married woman myself', the devar said.

(Narayan 2005: 73–74)

Thus, the woman is told bluntly by her husband's brother (*devar*) that he is unable to support her. Later in the song, people of her father's house, the father himself, the brother and the mother, all refuse one by one to help her on some pretext or the other. Her brother's wife (*bhauja*) plainly tells her, 'O Nand, the loaf that I might give you, will be eaten by my children.'

In some songs other members of an immigrant's family are also shown to be undergoing hardships, together with his wife. A *poorbi* tells this very type of *bidesia* effect:

The parrot flew and reached Calcutta.
And reaching there he sat on the master's turban
Taking off his turban the master seated him on the thigh
'Tell O' parrot, the welfare of my home
Your mother husks corn, your sister grinds,
And your wife has put up to shop.'

(Narayan 2005: 74)

A man who stays away for a long time is likely to develop relations with some other woman. Many songs sung by women express this apprehension and warn men to be careful not to fall prey to the machinations of the women of Calcutta.

This fear psychosis syndrome of a co-wife usually recurs in the Bhojpuri folklore:

Wheat was sown but ankari grew
My lord laments sitting on the road
O Lord, do not lament, do not, kill yourself lamenting
I shall exchange ankari and grind wheat
My wife, you have become thin due to grinding and pounding
If you like I shall bring a maid for you
He went for a maid, but brought a co-wife.
How shall I undo this bargain of the co-wife.

(Narayan 2005: 75)

In many Bhojpuri folk songs, the migrant is asked the painful question why he left his native place. The replies of the migrants have been found in the folk songs of Fiji, Suriname and so on, which narrate the compulsions of the migrants that led to his migration.

The man was forced to leave his home because the crops had failed. We also find in the songs that people go to cities not because they are attracted by them but, in most cases, go only when they are unable to earn their livelihood in the village. In fact it appears that even when a man has left the countryside and lives in the city, he was sorry to have to do so. In the following *biraha*, an *ahir* (cowherd) laments the loss of his old surrounding and occupation:

> The watching of cows is gone
> The bath in the Ganges is gone
> The gathering under the Pakari tree is gone
> God has taken away all the three
> (Narayan 2005: 76)

The folk songs pertaining to the separation of human bonds not only merely describe the loneliness of the separated but also express various social cultural animosities within and without the family. This *bidesia* tradition is continuing even today, and consequently the same voices of pain and separation can be heard in the folklores of Bhojpuri region.

The relatives of the migrants addressed them as *bidesia* (outsiders), and this sense of being an outsider has been accepted as a psychological pain by the migrants with deep anguish. Therefore their feelings are articulated with the same sense of an outsider uprooted from his place of origin and entertaining the desire to return to it. Such a context is clearly visible in the folk songs of Bhojpuri residents in Fiji:

> *Firangi ke rajua maa chhuta mora desua se*
> *Gori sarkar chali chal re bidesia*
> *Bholi hame dekh arakati bharamaya ho*
> *kalkatta paar Jao paanch Sal re Bidesia*
> *Dipua maa laye pakrayo kagadua ho*
> *Anguthwa lagaye dindar re bidesia*
> *Kudari kurwal dono hathua mein hamre ho*
> *Gham maa pasina bahae re bidesia.*
> (Narayan 2005: 94)

*Translation*

It was during the British rule, that we left our land.
Under a capricious design of theirs, credulous middleman allured us to go to the land away from Calcutta for a period of five years.

On a blank paper we were asked to put our thumb impressions, which in fact was a deal of labour supply; thus we became labourers.

Taking *kudari* (spade) and *kurwal* (sickle) in our hands, the sweat of our body flowed in their lands under the heat of the sun.

The inhabitants of the Bhojpuri region were emotionally fragmented because on the one hand they had to bear the pain of separation from their native land, and on the other the element of being a foreigner against their will put them in the trauma of struggle within their past and present. We find in them the presence of both *desia* (nativity) and *bidesia* (outsidedness). Thus the diasporic identity is an identity of conflict and alienation, separation on the one hand and the absence of belongingness on the other. In many folk songs one comes across the same self complaining to himself and also arguing with himself.

The folk psyche of Bhojpuri region perceives this overseas migration as imprisonment of *kala pani* for her people. The folklore of migrants also describes this migration as imprisonment of *kalapani*.

*Pal Ke Jahajua maa roi-dhoi paithi ho*
*Kaise hoi kala pani paar re videsia*
*Jiyara diae Ghat Kyan nahi aae ho'*
*bita din kal bhae maas re videsia.*
           (Narayan 2005: 79)

*Translation*

Weeping and sitting in the ship with a sail,
anxious to know the journey to the fearful place
the heart is sinking and the mind is disturbed
as the destination is not visible.

The word *kala pani* represents prison in Andaman island during the colonial time, but in the folk psyche, it has come to acquire multiple meanings:

1   Imprisonments at a particular isolated and terrifying place.
2   A place where the drinking water was heavily polluted and its consumption would necessarily lead to death. Therefore it was a place of no return.
3   *Kala pani* means being banished from one's land.

However, in all these meanings there are two common implications. These are first, punishment for engaging in anti-British activities on a large scale, and second a severe punishment inflicted on those accused of treason. Hence *kala pani* represents a highly frightening punishment at a distant place from where there would be no news from anywhere.

Thus Bhojpuri folk psyche perceives *kala pani* as an exile and metaphor of colonial reign of terror. This metaphor used in the *poorbi* and *kajari* songs reveals the state of pain and anguish of Bhojpuri folk due to this overseas migration. The migrants perceived this migration as forced migration also:

*Ab Se Khabardar raho bhai*
*Teri bigari baat ban Jai*
*kalkatte mein bharati Karke bhej diye jab bhai*
*laye utare surinam mein dipu mein bhat khawai*
*Teen mahine Jalyana Safar mein lakh Jhapere khai*
*Shri Ram nagar ki charcha karake surinam giye pahunchai*
*hot savera nam bulakar bakara ne baat sunai*
*Paanch saal contrak kaat lo fir bharat dev pahunchai*
*Ranga Kat liye hath mein lekar jangal kato jai*
*Chiuta chiuti katan lage hay hay chillayee*
*jangal kante, koko kante jana diye banai*
*Ekh kaat pakai ke hamne shuku rudiye banai*
*Kangak kaatkar kuch longon ne bharat gaye parai*
*Rah gaye jo surinam mein apna apna ghar basai*
*Chautis hazar bharati aaye the bara hazar gai Lautai*
*Baaies hajar jo bache the charo ub Deth saou hajar ho jai*
*atharah saou tihatar se unnis saou solah tak chousath jalyan yahan bhai*
*jahaji bankar aaye the sab bankar rahe jahaji bhai*
*bharti surinam mein aaye hindu, muslim, sikh, isayee*
*bhagya kahoo, durbhagya kahoo, kishore samajh mein kuchh nahi aai.*

(Narayan 2005: 80)

*Translation*

Be careful, your bad fortune will come to an end.
From Kalkatta, we were sent to a depot in Suriname where we were fed rice.
After a three month long difficult journey by ship, we reached Suriname, which we had earlier taken to be Shri Ram's land.
As soon as it is morning, the bakara (white owner), called us and promised to send us back to India after completing the five year contract.
34,000 Indians came here and 12,000 have already gone back.

Between 1873 and 1926, 64 ships came here.
We came here as 'jahaji', and remained as 'jahaji brothers'.
Kishor (the poet) does not know whether to call it his good luck or bad luck.

(This song describes the journey of a migrant labourer to Suriname, from his recruitment at a depot in Calcutta, to his arrival at the destination point, and the adverse circumstances that he is forced to experience at the plantation. He is lamenting at his fate, which has caused this situation.)

A heart-breaking pain for the person who has been compelled to go to *kala pani* is expressed very pathetically in a folk song composed by a dancer of Varanasi named Sundari Vaishya, near about 1880, is as follows:

*Aare rama nagar naiya Jala kalapania re hari*
*Sabhaket nala Jala kasi ho bisesar rama*
*nagar naia jala kalapania re hari.*
(ibid: 81)

*Translation*

O Rama, the boat of *Nagar* (a wrestler who transformed himself
 into a freedom fighter) is going to *kala pani*, O Hari.
Everybody's boat is going to Kasi and Bisesar, O Rama,
but *Nagar's* boat is going to *kala pani*, O Hari.

In Bhojpuri folk consciousness, there is an imagined perception that *kala pani* is located in the East. The following folk song suggests it as follows:

*Purub ke desawa se aile topiwalawa rama*
*dera dale sunder ke aanganawa re hari*
*Bhari bhari kurul sona debo topiwalawa rama*
*Nagar naiyya mat le ja kalapaniya re hari.*
(ibid: 82)

*Translation*

A *topiwala* (agent) has come from *purub*, O Rama
and has planted himself in the courtyard of a beautiful woman
 (called Sundar).
I will give you (*topiwala*) a lot of gold, O Rama,
but please do not take *Nagar* to *kala pani*, O Hari.

There is a belief in Bhojpuri folk consciousness that everyone who leaves his or her place goes to the countries of *purub* (east). In fact Calcutta is situated in *purub*. Most of them go to Assam, Mauritius, Fiji and so on via Calcutta. Not only is there a *kala pani* but it is also located in *purub*. *Topiwala* (*Arkatiya, dalal*) (agents of Colonial Sugar Refinery Company (CSRC) and others used to come from *purub* (east) and take *Nagars* (a wrestler of Banaras) towards *kala pani*. The ship also multiplies the degree of pain because it was used to take the beloved to the *kala pani*. Around 1899 when the above-mentioned song was composed, the ship was perceived as an enemy for those who were left behind. In 1920, the rail emerged as a greater enemy for them:

> *Railiya Sawatiya mor salyan ke lele Jaye*
> *Pahile railiya o kare bad sawatiya*
> *Railiya Sawatiya, more saiya ke lele Jaye*
> (Narayan 2005: 83)

*Translation*

Railways are like my husband's second wife, which takes him away.

## *Bidesia nautanki* and **Bhikhari Thakur**

One of the leading aspects of the *bidesia* folk culture was the *bidesia nautanki* or *bidesia* folk theatre tradition developed by Bhikhari Thakur, who converted the *bidesia* folk music tradition into a folk theatre tradition. His *bidesia* theatre was composed and staged in 1912, but was published in 1917. In earlier compositions like a composition of Sri Ram Sakal Pathak Dwijram called *Sundari Vilap* composed in 1896 and the composition by Shri Nath Sharan in 1912 called (*Pyari Sundari Viyog*), *bidesia* was used only as an address. Bhikhari Thakur's folk theatres were filled with *bidesia* songs and music, in which the folk tradition developed by Dwijram in the *bidesia* style was included. The *bidesia* of Dwijram and the *bidesia* of Bhikhari Thakur were similar because they both described the anguish caused by leaving the family and native land behind by migrants of the Bhojpuri region. The only difference is that while the *bidesia* folk songs composed by Dwijram describe the migration to foreign lands like Surinam, Fiji and Mauritius, for Bhikhari Thakur, Calcutta represents a place where there is internal migration by the migrants. In addition he describes the external migration to overseas countries. The common people called the songs in these theatres '*bidesia* songs'. The style used by Bhikhari Thakur became so popular that people started calling other *nautankis* also *bidesia*. Not only this, other theatre companies also started enacting *bidesia* theatres. Like *jatra* and *kirtaniya* in Bengal; *raas, jhoomar* and *dhola* in Rajasthan; *bhavai* in Gujarat; *larite* and *tamasha* in Maharashtra; *raas, nautanki, swang* and *bhand* in Awadhi, Poorvi, Braj, Hindi and Khari Boli, *bidesia* became the popular folk theatre style of the Bhojpuri region. Before this there was no other individual folk theatre style in the Bhojpuri region. The only folk style was the dance of the *netua* (the Nat community) on the beats of the dhol, *pakhawaj* (an Indian barrel-shaped two-headed drum), *jhal* (Hindu musical brass cymbal), *kartal* (percussion instrument of India used in devotional/folk songs) and *jori* (a Sikh Musical instrument also known as the Punjabi Pakhawaj), the *dhobi* folkdance and the *jogira* folk dance style. Bhikhari Thakur assimilated many features of the *godh* dance and the *jogira* style in his *bidesia* theatre. He was also inspired by the *jatra* folk theatre style of Bengal (Majumder 2010: 153–154).

*Bidesia* is dominantly a style involving songs and dances. All characters, from the king to the yogi, sing and dance on the stage. The characters of the *bidesia* theatre enter the stage singing and then start dancing on the beats of the *duggi*. Apart from the musical instruments of the *Parsi* theatre and other folk theatres, the dholak, sarangi, harmonium, *jhaal, kartal* and *jori* are compulsory in the *bidesia* theatres. There are no curtains or stage, and the theatres are usually acted on benches inside shamianas or on wooden planks on a dhurrie, under the sky. Bhikhari Thakur was also the first person to cast male actors in female roles wearing feminine clothes in the *bidesia* folk theatre (ibid: 154).

The *bidesia* plays are a mixture of prose and poetry. The entire play is filled with *bidesia* songs. The songs are composed on folk tunes. Based on *lorikayan, jantsari, sorthi, birha, barahmasa, poorvi, alha, pachra, kunvar bijai, nirgun, chaupai, kavita, chaubisa* and other folk music, the *bidesia* songs touch the hearts of the listeners (ibid).

The storyline of the plays is usually related to the sorrow of a young bride whose husband has been forced to leave her back in the village and go to *pardes* or foreign land to look for a job. It develops in the form of Sundari sending a message through a messenger to her husband and telling the messenger to bring him back to the village after releasing him from the clutches of another woman in the city. The entire story develops in such a fashion that even the most stonehearted person will feel like crying. *Bidesia* theatres, however, not only are the story of grieving young women but also narrate the feelings of young men who return to their village after roaming hither and thither in the city, looking for work (ibid).

There are usually four characters in this folk theatre style: The *bidesi*, *pyari* Sundari, *Randi* (other woman), and the *batohi* (messenger). The *sutradhar* or narrator, from time to time, indicates the relevance of the story and also the happenings of the story through dance and narration. All the actors sit on the stage, and when their turn comes, they stand up and act their role.

They use very little make-up. Sometimes a character may mingle with the audience and go up to the stage from there. Right from the beginning, the characters are closely linked to the audience. The theatre begins with *mangalacharan* or prayer to the gods. After that the *sutradhar* comes on the stage and familiarizes the audience with the characters, storyline and the import of the play. The tone and style of the *sutradhar* is such that the audience gets easily moved. Till Bhikhari Thakur was alive, he used to enact the role of the *sutradhar*. The role of the *sutradhar* is like that of a modern poet (ibid: 154–155).

The second most important role in these theatres is that of the *vidushak* (*labaar*). In between the play, the *labaar* enters the stage and entertains the audience with small jokes. The jokes were meant for entertainment, but alongside, they were a satire on the malpractices and superstitions prevalent in the society. Just before a tragic scene was about to be enacted, in the tradition established by Bhikhari Thakur, the *labaar* would come on stage and narrate a funny joke. In this manner, on the one hand the audience would be in splits of laughter, and on the other, they were mentally prepared for the anticipated tragic scene. In the *bidesia* style, tragedy and comedy went hand in hand. Bhikhari Thakur was the first to cast young, talented boys of the Bhojpuri region in female roles and popularize the *launda* dance. In this manner he also incorporated characters like *launda* and *labaar* in the *bidesia* folk theatre (ibid: 155).

The other character, the Sundari, is full of anguish because of the impact of the migration of the *bidesia*. This anguish is evident in the following folk song:

> *Tohre karanwa paranwa dukhit bate*
> *Daya kake darsan de d ho balamua*
> (Bhikhari Thakur)
> (Yadav and Singh (ed.) 2005: 37)

*Translation*

My heart is full of sadness because of you.
Kindly show yourself to me, O my beloved.

The *batohi* or the messenger, who was another important character in the *bidesia* theatre, was the one to whom the wife narrated her sorrow, which she requested him to convey to her migrant husband (Majumder 2010: 155).

The *bidesia* folk theatre became popular in the Bhojpuri region for many reasons. The most important one was that the songs portrayed the miseries of the common people like drought and famine, which compelled their migration to other cities in search of jobs. Added to this was the pressure from the colonialists, who forced them to go to Trinidad, Mauritius, Fiji, Suriname and so on as indentured labourers. The narration of these regular occurrences in the *bidesia* plays touched a common chord in the hearts of all the audience. The interspersion of comic relief and satire on the existing system established the *bidesia* plays as an extremely popular form of folk art and culture. These plays were also a statement on the existing social dichotomies and the process of displacement of the Bhojpuri migrants. Contemporary Hindi theatre has now started adopting the *bidesia* folk tradition. Kala Sangam of Patna, in its play *Harikesh Muluk* and the play *Mati Gadi* by the Mrichchh Katikam Rupantaran, gained immense popularity by using the *bidesia* folk theatre style (ibid: 155–156).

## *Bidesia* folk culture in Suriname

### *Reply of* bidesia *question in songs and literature*

An interesting dimension of the migration from the Bhojpuri region is that parallel to the *bidesia* folk tradition that evolved in the Bhojpuri region of India, similar folk traditions also emerged in the countries to which the migrants went. These folk cultural traditions were the outcome of the gushing out of the inner sorrow of the migrants at leaving their loved ones and their country behind. They worked as support systems to sustain the migrants during the long stormy journeys and in their life at the destination points and gave them inner strength to face the adverse circumstances. If the *bidesia* folklore composed in the Bhojpuri region is placed before the *bidesia* folk songs composed in places like Fiji, Suriname and Mauritius, they will sound like emotional questions and answers of this major socio-historical event. The feelings of the family members of the Bhojpuri migrants became stronger and stronger that their loved one had left them due to some mistake or crime committed by them. This is evident when the common people of the Bhojpuri region ask the question (ibid: 156):

*Kai kaili chukwa ki chhorala mulukawa tu*
*Kahala na dilwa ke haliya balamu*
*Saanvli suratiya saalat bate chhatiya mein*
*Eko nahi patiya bhejal balmua*
*Kaun nagariya dagariya mein piya mor*
*Karat Hoib ghar baas ho balmua*
*Kahat bhikhari nai aas naikhe eko pai*
*Hamra se hokhe ke deedar ho balmua*
                    (Bhikhari Thakur)
                              (ibid)

*Translation*

What crime have I committed that you left the country and did not tell me your feelings before leaving?
I keep remembering your face in my heart, sitting on my terrace. But you did not even send me a letter.
I don't know in which country and in which road my beloved is now living in.
*Bhikhari Nai* (barber) is saying that there are no hopes that the beloved will ever return.

In the songs composed at the destination points, the *bidesia* (migrant) himself narrates the pain and sorrow he feels at being displaced from his homeland. The migrants agree with the complaints of the Bhojpuri people that they left their homeland in search of money. They say that they did not want to leave their homeland, but compulsions led them to do so. One folk song sung by the migrants in Suriname depicts their misery (ibid: 157).

*Ab se khabar dar raho bhai*
*Teri bigri baat banjai*
*Kalkatte mein bharti karke bhej diye jab bhai*
*laye utare surinam mein dipu mein bhat khawai*
*Teen mahine jalyan safar mein lakh jhapere khai*
*Shri ram nagar ki charcha karke surinam giye pahunchai*
*Hot savera nam bulakar bakara ne baat sunai*
*Paanch saal contrak kat lo fir bharat dev pahunchai*
*chautis hazar bharati aae the bara hazar gaye lautai*
*1873 se 1926 tak chausat jalyan yaha bhai*
*jahaji bankar aye the, sab bankar rahe jahaji bhai*
*Bhagya kahun, durbhagya kahun, kishor samajh mein kuchh nahi aai.*

(Narayan 2005: 96–97)

*Translation*

Be careful, your bad fortune will come to an end.
From Calcutta, we were sent to a depot in Suriname where we were fed rice.
After a three-month long difficult journey by ship, we reached Suriname, which we had earlier taken to be Shri Ram's land.

As soon as it is morning, the *bakara* (white owner) called us and promised to send us back to India after completing the five-year contract.
34,000 Indians came here and 12,000 have already gone back.
Between 1873 and 1926, sixty-four ships came here.
We came here as *jahaji* and remained as '*jahaji* brothers'.
Kishor (the poet) does not know whether to call it his good luck or bad luck.

The composer of this song was Pt Kishor Mahtab Singh, who is a famous folk singer of Suriname. Another *bidesia* song composed in Suriname is the following (Majumder 2010: 158):

*Chhor aili hindustanwa babuwa, petwa ke liye*
*Padli bharam mein, chhutal patna ke saharwa*
*Chhut gaili ganga maiya ke ancharwa*
*Na hi manli ekobaba bhaiya ke kahanwa*
*Babua petwa ke liye*
                              (Narayan 2005: 98)

*Translation*

We left Hindustan to satisfy our stomach.
We were convinced by the sweet words of the *dalal* (*arkatiya*) and in the process were separated from Patna and the Ganga River.
We did not listen to our elders, but came here because of our stomach.

These and other such songs composed in all the Caribbean countries to which the migrants went depict the emotional loss caused to them. In Suriname every year a festival is held at the Lala Rukh Mahasagar (named after the first ship that brought the Hindustanis to Suriname) to remember the coming of the forefathers where their sorrow and anguish is expressed through the folk songs sung there (Majumder 2010: 158).

In addition to the folk songs, many poems were written that narrated the pain of the *bidesias*. The following two poems are from Amarsingh Raman's collection *Phulon ke Panchi* (Bird of Flowers), printed in 1984 in Delhi (India) and published by Sanatan Dharm Mahasabha, Paramaribo. They are exemplary poems on 'migrant's memory' (*Pravásí Yádgár*: 32) and on 'separation (pain) of immigrants' (*Pravásí Viraha*: 47) (ibid).

*Pravásí Yádgár*

*Vahi dinvá jab yád ávelá, ankhiyá me bharelá páni re.*

*Hindustán se bhágkar aili, yahi hai apni kaháni re,*
*bhái chutá, báp chutá, aur chuti mahatári re.*
*Arkatiyá khub bharmavlis, kahai paisá kamaibu bhar-bhar tháli re,*
*vahi cakkar má par gaili, bacvá yád áy gail náni re.*

*'Mariyá bhaish' ke jangal má biti mori javáni re,*
*tab bhi kamáy-kamáy ke larkan ke khub parhavli re.*
*Dákter, vakil, sestar, jaj, sipáhi, mestar sabká khub banavli re,*
*apná socá kuch na bhavá, bacvá sab par gavá páni me.*

*bitiyá bhágá, betavá bhágá, hoylán ki rájdháni me,*
*biná mehnat ke máng kar kháte hain is bhari javáni me.*
*Ham to sarnamvá ke jangal kát-kát kar unnati khub karavli re,*
*jab sukh karne ká bariyá ává, tab yahi dashá ham pavli re.*

*Translation*

*Immigrant's memory*

When that day comes to mind, the eyes get filled with water,
Fleeing Hindustan, I've come (here) – this is my personal story.
Brother got separated, father got separated and my wife got
    separated.
The recruiter deceived me badly, saying that I would make much
    money.
I got stuck into that web, O dear, and suffered tremendous pain.

In the jungle of [plantation] Mariënbosch I passed my youth.
Nevertheless, I could educate my children well by hard work.
I made them doctor, lawyer, nurse, judge, police and teacher.
[But] whatever I had in mind, nothing came out, all failed,
    O dear!

Daughters as well as sons fled to the capital of Holland.
In the prime of youth they do not work but live on alms.
I for one have made ample progress by cutting the jungle of
    Surinam.
When came the time to enjoy, I faced this situation.

*Pravásí Viraha*

*Chor aili Hindustánavá babuvá petavá ke liye,
Chorali maiyá, bappá, bandhu, sárá parivárvá,
ki chutal milan kar ásh.*

*Parli bharam me, chutal Patná ke shaharavá,
chut gaile pyári Gangá maiyá ke ancaravá,
náhi mánli ekau bábá bhaiyá ke kahanavá,
babuvá petavá ke liye.*

*Chor aili Hindustánavá babuvá petavá ke liye,
rote hoihain joru aur god ke gadelavá,
ki kari-kari daduvá ke ásh.
Phuti gaile karam, ki tuti gaile nátavá,
samujhi-samujhi man roye kalkatavá,
jiyará ke bujháve káhi gáve lagali gánavá,
babuvá petavá ke liye.*

*Chor aili Hindustánavá babuvá petavá ke liye,
svarg se jahán morá chutal ved aur puránavá,
ki hoygá dharma násh.
Rám-dhám chut gaile, milá banbasavá,
cunni-khuddi kháy-kháy, kátli hai ghásavá,
manjhá ke gulámi karli to milal dui dánavá,
babuvá petavá ke liye.*

*Chor aili Hindustánavá babuvá petavá ke liye.*


*Translation*

Separation (pain) of Immigrants

I've left Hindustan, O dear, for stomach's sake,
left mother, father, relatives, the whole family,
[even] the hope of [ever] meeting them [again] has faded away.

I became deluded [which] separated me from the city of Patna,
I have lost the lovely care of Mother Ganges,
I did not heed to [any of] father's and brother's advices.
O dear, for stomach's sake . . .

I've left Hindustan, . . .
Must be crying [my] partner and baby in the lap,
[desperately] hoping [to see] their beloved one (*dadu*).
Destroyed is my destiny, snatched are my family ties.
Remembering (this) the mind cries for Calcutta.
For cooling the heart, why do I start singing the song: 'O dear, for stomach's sake.'

I've left Hindustan, . . .
I've lost a 'world' like Heaven, the Veda-s and Purána-s,
And that [consequently my] religion will vanish!
I have lost [India,] the abode of Ráma
And found [instead Surinam, i.e. an] exile in the forest!

Feeding on morsels, I've cut grass,
Did slavery for the lord (*manjhá*), then got some food.
O dear, for stomach's sake
I've left Hindustan, O dear, for stomach's sake.

### Hindustani music in Suriname

Music and songs have always been powerful tools of cultural expression for people, especially those who are unable to put down their anguish in words. The same holds true of the Hindustanis of Suriname, most of whom were illiterate when they went to Suriname. The deep pain and sorrow in their hearts led to the creation of a rich cultural heritage of music and songs in Suriname that were based on the folk culture of the Bhojpuri region that they took along with them in their cultural baggage. Apart from some songs in a typical *bidesiá* style that conveyed the personal sense of bereavement and loss in an excellent way, there were some other styles such as the traditional *sohar* and *biraha* that were popular genres of folk music in the Bhojpuri region, which were used to render compositions with comparable *bidesiá* content. The entire indentureship period was characterized by the maintenance of ritual, folk and traditional songs like the *alha, pachara, marsiya,* qawwali, *nazam, Ramayana,* bhajan, *khajari-bhajan,* kirtan, *sohar, biraha* and so on. Around 1920 in the post-indenture period a folk music evolved in Suriname among the Hindustanis, which was the *baithak-gana*. With the evolution of this form, some of the earlier folk genres like *tajiya, alha* and *pachara* gradually disappeared. The peak phase of *baithak-gana* was between 1920 and 1950, during which this genre emerged and developed. The *baithak-gana* was widely popular and enjoyed at weddings and other socio-religious

*Figure 4.1* Hindustani Musicians during a Wedding Party in Suriname, Posing with Their Instruments Sarangi, *Dantal* and Dhol. Photograph: J. Dzn. Blaauboer 1952. Collection Tropenmuseum 10020893

gatherings. See figure 4.1. The musicians and the singer, along with other invited artists, traditionally perform on the floor seated in a circular or 'U' formation. While there are speculations on the origin of *baithak-gana*, little can be said with certainty on this matter, except perhaps that it accommodates both North Indian and Caribbean elements. The earliest form of this music has a serious character, and perhaps on that account it is qualified as 'classical' as compared with Western classical music. The songs are usually inspired by the religion and culture of the Hindustanis and comprise both Hindus and Muslims. These songs usually reflect a serious, austere and religious sentiment, inspired by the Hindu epics such as *Ramayana* and *Mahabharata*, reflecting the exploits of religious figures such as Rama, Krishna, Sita and Hanuman. Another popular category of songs came from history (*itihasa*) and mythology (*purana*). A notable characteristic of this music was the element of competition or criticism (*khandan* and *shastrartha*). The format of the music performance was that of a dialogue, or *sawal-jawab*, which required a 'question' or proposition to be met with an appropriate 'response' fully in line with the theme of the question. This meant that the participating singers had to have a good command on a vast repertoire of religious, cultural, historical and mythological songs (Majumder 2010: 161, 163).

Between 1950 and 1990 the culture of modernity, westernization and creolization transformed the semi-classical *baithak-gana* into what now had come to be known as orchestra music, mainly due to further influences of Western and Hindi pop (ibid). One of the first orchestras was the Indian Orchestra. During the 1950s until the second half of the 1970s we had both genres: the modern orchestra and the *baithak-gana*. *Baithak-gana* groups were promoted by some radio stations by giving them a free platform for performances in the studio. The radio programmes were also aimed for Caribbean audience outside Suriname.

Some orchestras such as the Oranje Band and Sohani Orchestra initially retained some of the traditional instruments such as the dholak and harmonium, but with the introduction of electric amplification they were also gradually disposed or, in fact, substituted by the drum and electric organ, respectively. Finally, the inclusion of 'non-Indian' musical instruments such as electric instruments (guitars and organs), brass, drum, tambourines, maracas, congas and bongos completed the transformation of the 'semi-classical' into full-blown modern bands, completely dominated by Western ('non-Indian') en Afro-musical instruments, melodies and rhythms. A relatively early example is Bhikhari Thakur's song *awo mere yaro, milkar gawo gana, aur khawo baka bana* (Come, my friends, let's sing together, and eat fried bananas.). In this song only the lyric is in Hindi, whereas the music provided by Sohani Orchestra is bereft of Indian elements and replete with Caribbean elements such as steel band brass and percussion sections. The lyrics of the songs often reflected the general state of mind of the Hindustanis. The music also functioned as an instrument for spreading news and important local events. Besides being a means of musical entertainment, *baithak-gana* became an important vehicle for conveying satire and criticism on local socio-cultural and political developments. For example, in the post-indenture times, Indian immigrants often became the victim of exploitation and fraud as attested by a well-known lamentation on Miranda's scandalous abuse of their trust and faith (ibid: 163):[1]

| | |
|---|---|
| *Ab se khabardár raho bhái,* | From now on, be aware brother, |
| *tum par gam ki ghatá hai cháyi.* | a dark cloud of sorrow is hovering on you. |
| ... | |
| *Kauri-kauri paisa jore,* | Counting penny for penny, |
| *jore dhare ghar máhi,* | he saved some money at home. |
| *Paisa ke gathari sir par dharke,* | Putting the bunch of money on his head, |
| *Mirándá kantoro pahunchái.* | he carried it to the office of Miranda. |
| *Ab se khabardár raho bhái* | From now on, be aware O brother! |
| | |
| *Ley le pápá paisa dharle,* | Take it Father, keep the money, |
| *yehi hamáre kamái,* | this is my [lifetime] earning. |
| *Paise leke pápá Mirandá,* | Taking the money, Father Miranda, |
| *afsar papirá thamái.* | issued an official document. |
| *Ab se khabardár raho bhái* | From now on, ... |
| | |
| *Onnais sau unchás ke samay djab ái,* | When the year 1949 arrived, |
| *netá lekar jái* | he went with a local leader to a civil servant, and when the latter saw the document, he issued the warning, |
| *ab to khabardár raho bhái,* | from now on, ... |
| | |
| *Kantaro me paisa náhi,* | There is no money in the office, |
| *rowat ghar ko áyi,* | he came crying home. |
| *Hái, daiyá ham aisá janti,* | O God, would I've known this, |
| *larkan det parhai.* | I would have spent it on educating my children. |

However, the *baithak-gana* gradually gave way to a modern *chutney* phase, with the emergence of modern media such as radio, TV, cinemas and, most importantly, Bollywood film and music. The term *chutney* traditionally denoted light, fast and often ribald songs in Bhojpuri, a dialect of Hindi. *Chutney* songs were usually performed in playful rhythms of four-quarter and three-quarter beats such as *kaharva* and *dadra tala-s*. Originally *chutney* did not definitely meant dance music. In fact, the *chutney* style belonged to the category of listening music and was meant as a change or intermezzo to the heavy and austere atmosphere of the 'classical' styles like *dhurpad*, *thumri* or qawwalis. The contents should, therefore, be somewhat light and not heavy as those of the songs mentioned earlier. *Chutney* songs were most typically performed, often with lewd dancing, by women in sexually segregated contexts at weddings and childbirth festivities. Creole artists were invited to play in the bands and help arranging the compositions to rhythms of *kaseko, kawna,* calypso, *bobbling, speedy bobbling,* house, bhangra and so on. Thus far, these fusions proved to be very successful among youngsters. These attempts to mix so many different genres and rhythms from different parts of the world attest to recent processes of globalization. The people of Suriname and the Caribbean fully contributed to this development with their music. This process can perhaps be explained by the fact that in an environment where the colonial system gave the Creole culture ascendancy over Indian customs in almost the entire region, the survival of Indian culture, including its music, was under threat. In the Anglophone Caribbean as a whole, sometimes the survival of the music resists cultural oblivion. Amid a dominant Creole culture, the only solution for survival has obviously been to join them if you cannot beat them. This perhaps explains the survival of *chutney, chutney-soca* and other musical forms with English texts and Caribbean rhythms (Majumder 2010: 165).

Even at present *chutney* is one of the most popular music and dance forms of the Hindustani culture in the Caribbean. One of the most famous vocal representatives of this genre has been the late Ramdew Chaitoe. He has shown that at a time when in Suriname the local classical form of *baithak-gana* was disappearing, new life and vitality could be injected to it by preparing a creative cocktail of Bollywood and Caribbean beats. *Chutney*'s popularity, although growing, continues to be surpassed by that of Indian film music, which has dominated music culture in the Indo-Caribbean as in India itself. But there is good news for connoisseurs of Hindustani Surinamese music since *baithak-gana* is once again showing signs of revival due to the efforts of some Hindustani Surinamese musicians and patrons who are concerned about the extinction of their cultural heritage (ibid: 165–166).

## *Baithak-gana* in the Netherlands

With the massive migration of Hindustanis, many *baithak-gana* artists too left for the Netherlands,[2] whereas only just a few remained in the country.[3] Some people refer nostalgically to the pre-independence period as the time when all artists were still in Suriname and the post-independence period conversely as the era when most had settled in the Netherlands and left Suriname almost as a barren country, musically speaking, of course. The demographical reshuffle broke up numerous bands in Suriname, but, on the other hand, it created in the Netherlands a unique opportunity to form new ones, bringing together musicians from different parts of Suriname. It was in this relaxed and aspiring atmosphere that *baithak-gana* in the Netherlands flourished during 1975 and 1985. This period reached its peak with Ramdew Chaitoe, one of the last doyens of the classical *baithak-gana* (ibid: 166).

The sad demise of Ustad Ramdew Chaitoe heralded a period of decline and neglect of *baithak-gana* due to a decreased interest in the music. The new generation of Hindustanis who were brought up in the Netherlands was naturally influenced and attracted by modernities outside their own community such as Western and Hindi pop. This generation had come to consider the *baithak-gana* as old-fashioned and associated it with the older generation who couldn't let go of their old traditions and customs (ibid).

It was perhaps Ustad Ramdew Chaitoe who recognized this problem and actively tried to solve it. As an established musician, he could mark out a new path to attract the younger generation. In this respect he first made *baithak-gana* more attractive and accessible to youngsters by not singing only classical genres such as *dhurpad, thumri* and *langri*, but focusing on *chutney* songs such as *roj dekhila* (calypso) and *rate sapna* (*dadra*). Ramdew Chaitoe's campaign attracted a number of students such as Ardjoen Autar, Vinod Rakhan Roy Ramadhien and Shankar 'Chanderbose' Sewlal. Initially they pursued the classical repertoire but were ultimately forced to focus on *chutney* and further simplify the *baithak-gana* with a profusion of simple beats such as calypso and *keherwa*. Because of this modernism, Ramdew Chaitoe also attracted some criticism. This was what led him to revert in his final years to classical *baithak-gana* (ibid).

After his death his students further simplified the music of their master and established their own music and market. One such student was Hanif Rojan, who followed him and also focused on the classical style. Kenneth Rakhan, a virtuoso *dholaki*, produced digital music on a rather high level by dubbing dholak rhythms on the music of his mother, Bidjanwati Chaitoe (sister of late Ramdew Chaitoe, singer in Amar Deep). Shankar 'Chanderbose' Sewlal, on the other hand, made loops of dholak rhythms, which could be used further in recording and remixing modern *baithak-gana* and *chutney*. With the digital development, this generation of *baithak-gana* artists ultimately got connected with people who were already active in the digital scene.[4] With the employment of dholak and *dantal* rhythms, the modern bands and DJs presented a music that had recognizable elements from *baithak-gana*. Even though the traditional music as well as its musical instruments had long since disappeared from the modern bands, these experiments with dholak and *dantal* rhythms once again introduced *baithak-gana* spirit to a broader public. This idea has been picked up and fully exploited by Faziel Wagid Hosein from 'The Juniors', who, in a way, has reintroduced *baithak-gana* to the younger generations (ibid: 167). Hafiezkhan Wagid Hosein is a leading member of Sohani Orchestra and founder/leader of Mastana Orchestra. He is uncle and teacher of all the Wagid Hoeseins of the newer generation who became popular in the Netherlands. Their popular band is called 'The Juniors'.

After the departure of Ramdew Chaitoe, Krish Ramkhelawan became the most popular and influential singer/artist in Suriname. He has done a lot of work and is training younger musicians on his own. His group's name is 'Saathi'. He is very popular in Trinidad, and his CDs are often launched in Trinidad instead of Suriname.

### *Recent trends in* baithak-gana

The songs and lyrics were traditionally confined to weddings where only women sung them to entertain themselves. However, their commercial exploitation and exposition to the general public were met with criticism from women, especially when the popular singer Rameschander Bihari recorded his *kamrá kháli hai* (Majumder 2010: 167).

In recent years the introspection of Hindustanis in the Netherlands took a critical turn when local city councillor Rabin Baldewsing qualified the Hindustani community as 'Triple D', using thereby the abbreviation for 'three dimensional' (3D) as a pun for three indulgences or vices: the first D stands for *doksa*, that is for eating (duck); the second for *dansi* (dancing); and the third for *daru* (drinking). Feelings naturally run high, but after a while people like DJ Raga Meno placed things again into prospect by bluntly demanding that 'We need the curry of *doksa*' (*Ham mánge doksá ke suruwâ*) (ibid).[5]

One may even discern a post-modern *baithak-gana* period because in Suriname and the Netherlands there are numerous musicians who, besides singing *chutney* and other modern genres, revert to the classical *baithak-gana* (ibid).

The turbulent history of Indo-Caribbean people reveals that though they have gone through numerous ups and downs, they and thus their culture were able to survive, apparently by its suppleness and resiliency. In this regard, their music, *baithak-gana*, has played an undeniable role in expressing and preserving the culture. As an inseparable and concomitant component of that culture, it proved to be a reliable mirror that reflects the development of the culture. The second wave of Indian diaspora, this time moving Hindustanis from the Caribbean to the other parts of the world, has not only spread Indian culture further to Europe, United States and Canada but also globalized their precious music, *baithak-gana* (ibid: 168).

### Indo-Surinamese drama

Traditionally, each village community had its own drama group, which performed during religious feasts. According to Van Kempen IV (2003: 100), such a group acted as a protector and transmitter of traditional values and as such also exercised some authority on the community. He further believes that with the improving communication between the villages and the contacts with other cultures, the village drama gradually started to decline (Majumder 2010: 168).

In the 1920s the first historical pieces were performed, based on dramatical works of Indians, but adapted by Surinamese authors to their local situations. Ramdew Raghoebier mentions that in those days in Middenpad van Kwatta a group led by Oedit Bhawanigoelam staged plays on gods and kings such as *Indra Sabha* and *Rupbasant* (see Raghoebier 1987: 78–87; Van Kempen IV 2003: 100). Raghoebier mentions many pieces, but it is not clear which pieces are direct renditions of the great epics, which are inspired by that material but adapted by Indian authors, and which one of them are indeed written by Surinamese authors (ibid., n. 494). *Indra Sabha*, for example, is known to be written in India in 1853 by Agba Hasan Amanat, but Raghoebier (1987: 81) incorrectly ascribes *Indra Sabha* and *Rupbasant* to Oedit Bhawanigoelam, perhaps because the tasks of writer, director and editor were not clearly defined (ibid., n. 495). Van Kempen (ibid.) further records only one performance of *Rupbasant* in April 1946 (DWT 4470/17–4–1946). Until World War II *Rupbasant* remained the most popular secular drama among the Hindustanis (ibid.).[6]

As a matter of fact, the plays were usually sponsored by well-to-do people of the community. Van Kempen (IV: 101) mentions one such eminent person, namely Ram Adhin (b. around 1876 near Allahabad, d. 1943),[7] who organized on plantation Ornamibo (*Sarnami*: Nainibog) *Satnarainkatha-s*, devotional gatherings with hundreds of participants, and at the end of which pieces with religious purport were performed such as *Raja Harischandra, Gopichand, Mordhvaj* and *Pahlad-Sangit*. These plays were staged in the open air against a screen put up as a decor, of which the ropes were attached to 'Bols' (*Jenever*) bottles, which were brought by the visitors. The plays, full of music and dance, were performed exclusively by men and lasted for the whole night. According to Van Kempen (IV: 101) amusement was the prime aim of this kind of drama, but it has undoubtedly contributed much to the preservation of the Indian languages in Suriname (against other Caribbean countries such as Guyana and Trinidad where these languages have disappeared). This may be true to some extent, but Van Kempen seems to oversee the fact that in Suriname there was no government policy to promote a foreign language (i.e. Dutch or English) among the Asians or to discourage their mother tongue. He further adds that much of the knowledge of religion, literature, history, language and moral has been passed on by these pieces (ibid: 168–169).

After 1940, plays were more often staged on elevated grounds and lightings were improved. The means of transportations to the cinema halls/theatres were poor, so that drama remained a main source of entertainment in the districts. With the independence of India (1947), its active policy to export Indian culture also increased. At the same time the pieces received a stronger Surinamese form: texts were simplified, the *Sarnami* gained ground on Hindi and local themes were touched upon (ibid: 169).

From the long list of plays mentioned by Raghoebier, one can at least conclude that the majority of the plays were still based on the material from the old Indian literature with a religious slant, though occasionally a piece occurred with a topical content such as *Achut Uddhar* ('emancipation of the untouchables') from Chedie 'Bahauw' Jhinkoe, a piece, as already indicated by the title, that criticizes the caste system (Raghoebier 1987: 85–87).[8] From these play writers only Chandramohan Randjitsingh made name also as a poet.

Hindustani drama groups appeared on the stages of Paramaribo theatres only after World War II. On 14 November 1948, a Guyanese party led by Dr Singh Jr, along with some citizens of Suriname, staged in theatre Luxor a play called *Gora*, after a novel of Rabindranath Tagore. The play was not reviewed very positively but managed to usher the Hindustani community into the theatre (DS 6472/16–11–1948) (ibid: 169–170).

In July 1953 the drama party of the Cultural Centre of Suriname (CCS), under the direction of Marcelle Joseph, staged into seven acts the Indian play *Shakuntala* by Kalidasa (with Bea Vianen as one of the actors). This was the first time when a Surinamese group presented a big Indian play as a production of the regular drama in a city theatre. It was not a spectacular piece with music and dance, but a static piece with complicated text. As observed by the *Surinamer*, 'The interesting experiment required courage from, our co-citizens of Indic descent, who are far less used to plays, than the rest of our population' (DS 7191/9–7–1953). Van Kempen (2003, IV: 102) further mentions that a number of Biblical plays staged by Christian organizations: *Yosaph aur uske bhai* (Joseph and his brothers) 1949 and more. The *Evangelische Broedergemeente* (Moravian Church) published a number of Biblical stories in *Sarnami* in a magazine called *Kroes kie Rooshnie* (Nr 6/8 Nov. 1956). However, these publications had no codifying effect on the language as they did in the Sranan Tongo (ibid. IV: 143; Damsteegt 1990: 25). The folk theatre of the Hindustanis, like that of other ethnic groups, also attracted many spectators. Goeroedath Kallasingh's *Ghar ke Bhed* (family secrets) was staged more than thirty times and his *Merie doesrie biwi* (my second wife) forty-one times, and Ramnarain Gangadien's *Hai re Paisa* (money, O dear!) had sixty-three performances (Van Kempen IV: 286) (ibid: 170).

## Hindustani folk drama (1957–1975)

Till around 1975 it was custom among Hindus to present during wedding parties, a specially written *nautankí* for that occasion, a piece without any divisions in acts and performed by men. One of the most popular of this genre was *Annyai ka natija* (the results of injustice), a piece on the misery of evil, hailing from the estate Kroonenburg in Commewijne (Van Kempen IV 2003: 309) (ibid).[9]

The old epics of India remained popular as ever. The Ram Lila was staged every year, and Tulsidas was honoured with the piece *Tulsidas ki mahanta* (The Greatness of Tulsidas) of the Indian Mahatam Singh, performed by the students of the Hindi School of Shanti Dal in 1964. In 1975 a drama group under the direction of Ammersingh Raman staged his piece *Panchwatie*, in which he had adapted fragments from the *Ramayana*.[10] Also the *Mahabharata* has been an important point of reference for many playwrights. In this way Indraj Oemrawsing made a piece in four acts, *Panchaalie* (Parvati, the woman from Panchal) in which a fragment from the epic was transformed into theatre on the basis of a book of N.B. Acharya. This play was staged on August 1961 in Thalia by the Hindustani Student Dramagroup (*Hindostaanse Studenten Toneelgroep*) (ibid: 170–171).[11]

In this period four important developments took place in the field of Hindustani drama. First, slowly on, it became custom to let males as well as females play roles. The first pass forward of this development came from Mahatam Singh, since 1961, cultural attaché of the Indian Council for Cultural Relations. He began allowing boys as well as girls to sing together in choirs and who later also let them perform one-act plays, for example *Sundar Ras* (beauty elixir) in 1966. His influence has been enormous on playwrights such as Kallasingh (Van Kempen IV 2003: 310) (ibid: 171).

The second important development was that the Surinamese matter came to dominate the Indian matter. There came a preference for ordinary Surinamese mortals, instead of god-like nobles from the Indian dramatic literature. With certain references and citations, the Indian epics anyway almost always kept resounding, while the *Ramayana* and *Mahabharata* kept inspiring new historical performances. The continuity of tradition was thus not lost but got a new place in modern developments (ibid).

Directly related to this secularization of dramatic matter was the custom to perform the pieces completely in *Sarnami*, or in *Sarnami* alternated with Hindi whenever the situation demanded so. This development has undoubtedly led to a renewed engagement of the Hindustani public to theatre. Moreover, linguists such as Motilal Marhé and Theo Damsteegt believe that around 1970–1975 it was asserted that *Sarnami* was spoken on the stage of the theatre, but the authors stuck to what they considered correct in formal situations: Hindi (Van Kempen IV 2003: 311). The last important development was the application of decors. Often performances were held under corrugated sheds (*golfplaat*) against the background of a simple cloth for the period of the performances. Sometimes the performances were held in rice mills and recreation halls. But, gradually, the Hindustani folk drama also conquered theatres, the cinema halls and drama halls in the districts as well as the theatres of Paramaribo (ibid.).

Each year on 5 June, immigration day was the reason for cultural celebrations.[12] Several plays were written in that connection also. In this way, *Prawasie* (emigrant), a play in six acts, written by Usharbudh Arya (now: Swami Veda Bharati), was performed, in which the past, present and future of Hindustani immigrants are portrayed.[13] At the celebration of the centenary of immigration in 1973, film director Monisha Chatterjee and musician Arun Kumar Chatterjee from Delhi received an invitation from the Nationale Stichting Hindostaanse Immigratie (NSHI). The couple arranged the performance of *Krishnalila* (divine play of Krishna) in dance form in CCS and the performance of *Subah ka bhula* (it's never too late to repent)/*De verloren zoon*, a 'modern and realistic play for our present-day youth' (Van Kempen IV 2003: 312).

Monisha Chatterjee wrote a story of R.R. Jadnanansing in dialogue form, and Arun Kumar Chatterjee took the music on his account. The subject of the play was most remarkable for the commemoration of immigration: elders send their children for study to the Netherlands, as a result of which they get 'infected' by the modern world. A photo in *De Ware Tijd* of a father in a traditional dress, son in a suit and his girlfriend in a mini-dress leaves little to guess.[14] Another piece written for the same occasion placed the geography somewhat different, but the tendency was the same: in *Dost ya dushman* (friend or enemy) of Shyam Gangaram Pandey, the author wanted 'to send a word of caution to the inhabitants of the interior who are so eager to move to the big city' (Majumder 2010: 172).[15]

These subjects cover 99 per cent of the themes of texts of Hindustani plays. Apart from the authors mentioned earlier, Ramchander Bansidhar, Sierie Jagai, Chedie Jhinkoe, Balkishun Kartaram, Madho Ramkhelawan, Chandramohan Randjitsingh, Chotoe Sankatsingh, Rini Shtiam and Ramnarain Gangadien wrote plays based on Surinamese relations. The latter was quite successful with his play *Hai re paisa* (money O dear!), which was staged in 1973 at least sixty-three times in CSS and in almost all the districts; estimations say that about 30,000 people saw the play, that is about 10 per cent of the population (ibid.).[16]

The most important drama groups were those of the organization Hindustani Nauyuwak Sabha, which already existed around 1955; Kalamitra founded by R. Raghoebier in 1959; Jagrietie founded by G. Kallasingh in 1961 and the Jivan Jotie organization of Ramnarain Gangadien, founded in 1972. However, many groups avoided any form of documentation because of their limited reach and never sought publicity except by means of advertisement through Hindustani radio stations. In this regard, G. Kallasingh was an exception and that was not a coincidence: no other Hindustani playwright had consciously opted for such a broad national position (ibid).

In this chapter we have described the cultural productions that were created in the Bhojpuri region of India and in Suriname after the process of migration began. This description demonstrates eloquently that the pain caused by the phenomenon of overseas migration was so intense that it led to the evolution of a distinct folk culture called *bidesia* folk culture, both in India and in the Caribbean countries including Suriname. Since most of the migrants and their family members were illiterate, these cultural productions were the only means to express their anguish. Interestingly, while the musical productions in Suriname were heavily based on the folk culture of the Bhojpuri region of India in the initial period of the indentureship, gradually a hybrid form of Hindustani Surinamese music evolved and developed because of the influence of the other ethnic folk cultures in Suriname, especially the Creoles, which impacted strongly on the musical instruments and rhythm. Later, with the advent of modernization and westernization, the folk culture underwent further changes that led it away from the traditional folk music of the Bhojpuri region of India. Over the years these changes were compounded by the influence of Hindi film songs and music when they invaded Suriname in a big way through television, videos and DVDs. The result is the *chutney* music, which is highly popular among the Hindustani youth of both Suriname and the Netherlands. At present when there is a strong desire among the Hindustanis of both Suriname and the Netherlands to regain their links with their roots in India, an effort is under way to revive the lost glory of the traditional *baithak-gana* and also the folk dramas of the Hindustani Surinamese, which are based on the folk culture of that region. It remains to be seen how much the effort will bear fruit (ibid: 172–173).

### *Goeroepersad Niranjan*[17]

In the 1990s and early 2000s Goeroepersad Niranjan has been very active in writing and directing a number of popular plays. A number of them were also performed in the Netherlands. His plays were very simple on daily/common problems of the Surinamese society.

Born as the first son of his parents (Jankipersad Niriandjan and Mangri Gangpat) on the 5 November 1949, Goeroepersad Niranjan was the eldest in a family of seven children. Together with his family, he lived in the Rahemalbuiten area, in Wanica district. To support his parents financially, Goeroepersad had dropped out of the secondary school (MULO) and started a career at a young age as a tailor. His devotion and hard work paid off, and in the course of the years he established a renowned readymade clothing factory Paramount in the capital city Paramaribo. Because of his profession, he was nicknamed 'tailor' (*kleermaker*), and many famous artists and other prominent figures such as Kries Ramkhelawan, Robby Oeditram and Dr Nannan Panday belonged to his clientele. At the age of thirty, he got married to Sewranie Ramdjas and fathered five children.

Goeroepersad was a very well-known, polite, respected and well-liked person. Besides being a tailor, he followed Hindi classes, and after finishing his Hindi education successfully, he started teaching the language himself. He also taught how to write poetry (*kavita*) and devotional and cultural songs (bhajan and kirtan). In 1978 he became the secretary of the Social and Cultural Union, the Jagriti Foundation (*Stichting Jagriti*). His involvement in the social and cultural world and his desire to contribute to a better society inspired him to write. He started writing short dramas in 1980, which were played by talented youngsters from his own neighbourhood on social and cultural events such as Diwali, *Phagwa* and other occasions. His first drama brought out on national level was in 1990 and was named *Paisaaur Pyaar*. He immediately gained success, and the drama was performed more than fifteen times in Paramaribo and other districts such as Nickerie, Commewijne and Saramacca where Hindustanis are largely concentrated. His fame reached out internationally, and in 1996 he was invited to perform with his drama group in the Netherlands for the play *Nashakebaad*.

In the Netherlands as well, his drama was a major success attracting between 500 and 1,500 Hindustani people each time his group performed. Between 1996 and 2006 he wrote many plays and was invited to also perform in the Netherlands five more times. Some very famous dramas were titled *Jaisa Karni Waisa Bharni, Paisa aur Pyaar, Wah re Paisa, Karmka Phal, Nashake Baad, Ham aur Hemaar Paisa, Kabhie Khatta Kabhie Mietha* and the most successful one *Aurat Betjarie Kya Kare*. The last one was performed thirty-two times in Suriname and fifteen times in the Netherlands. Besides writing plays, Goeroepersad Nirandjan was a member and part of the advisory committee of the sportsclub Hindalaya. He also wrote and composed the music for an aeroplane crash in 1989 in Suriname in which more than 200 passengers died.

All of Goeroepersad's dramas were sold out because they contained a unique combination of folkloristic drama and comedy. Social and cultural values were very important to Goeroepersad, and he tried to promote them through his dramas in which he tackled, among other themes, egoism, greed, materialism, quackery, fraud, jealousy, alcoholism, oppression of women, disrespect towards elderly, criminality, bad relations between mothers-in-law and daughters-in-law and suicide. His dramas at the same time promoted belief in God, praying, the good of humanity, social deeds, religion, language (*Sarnami*/Hindi), honesty, hard work and education as a key to a better life, community and society.

Goeroepersad had another key component in his dramas that he brought in in a very unique way: comedy. His scenes created often hilarious situations, bringing laughter to both children and adults. After almost every performance, the drama group received standing ovation. Goeroepersad's drama (*natak*) has been of eminent importance to the Hindustani community in Suriname. To the people, the hardships of life could be left behind for a two-and-a-half hours of fun. The messages delivered were always appreciated by the public and often reiterated and lived in real-life situations at home and other social events. The themes of his drama were often discussed during radio programmes and presented in local newspapers. 'Drama', Goeroepersad said, is 'a part of our culture, we should never forget that. Through drama we can keep our values alive, we can promote them in a good way and continue the work of our forefathers because if we don't remember our social and cultural values, our religion, our roots, we don't have any identity.'

Goeroepersad died at the young age of fifty-seven, on 18 August 2006. But his ideas and teachings are brought forward by his disciples Sahienshadebie Ramdas, Perdiep Dodah and Ladi Lachimipersad who, after his death, continued with his legacy by writing and playing drama in the same spirit as they were taught. Their dramas are a reflection of their guru's values and are, in similar ways, receiving national and international success.

### *Bhojpuri and* Sarnami

Although the migration of indentured labourers from East India took place from many linguistic and cultural zones of Bihar and Uttar Pradesh like Bhojpuri, Magahi, Awadhi and Braj, Bhojpuri was the language that was most commonly used by the migrants after reaching their destination points in the various Caribbean countries. Bhojpuri shares its vocabulary with Sanskrit, Hindi, Urdu and other Indo-Aryan languages of northern India. Bhojpuri and several closely related languages, including Maithili and Magadhi, form a part of the eastern zone group of Indo-Aryan languages, which includes Bengali and Oriya. Bhojpuri is a very popular regional language spoken in parts of north-central and eastern India and is the native language of the western part of the state of Bihar, the north-western part of Jharkhand and the Purvanchal region of Uttar Pradesh, as well as in the adjoining area of southern plains of Nepal. In addition, the immense magnitude of migration from this region to a large number of places both in India and abroad since historical times has conferred a global status to it as the migrants have carried their language with them, which has helped to spread it in all parts of the world. However, even though Bhojpuri is spoken by a large number of people across the globe, the status of the Bhojpuri language in India has remained controversial since it was always looked upon as a dialect of Hindi and not a standard language in its own right. Even the government of India, while taking census, did not recognize it as an official language since until recently it was an oral language with a rich folk culture but without a literary form. With the spread of education in the Bhojpuri region, Bhojpuri has now developed a written form and both the *Kaithi* and the Devanagari script are used for writing Bhojpuri. Today in India, Bhojpuri language and culture, which was mainly confined to the rural regions of Bihar and East Uttar Pradesh, is fast on its way to attaining the status of a prestige language due to the growing popularity of Bhojpuri folk culture with its rustic rural flavour, among the Bhojpuri speakers spread out all over the country. These Bhojpuri speakers, many of whom are now in powerful and influential positions, who once disclaimed Bhojpuri language and culture preferring to claim Hindi as their literary language, are now proudly asserting their Bhojpuri roots. In addition to the oral folk culture that has become extremely popular among them, a literary culture is developing, with many novels, short stories and poems being written and composed in Bhojpuri. This is facilitating to make Bhojpuri a literary language like the other standard languages of India (Majumder 2010: 132–133).

Another major achievement of Bhojpuri is that today many Bhojpuri movies are being produced in Mumbai, the film city of India, that are drawing viewers from all sections of the society. Bhojpuri films were popular in India in the decade of the 1960s, but their viewership was restricted only to the lower strata of small cities and villages since the rural folk culture and values of the Bhojpuri region were not much appreciated by the growing middle and upper classes in big cities who found urban culture and values more alluring. Gradually the low-scale Bhojpuri film industry faded out, and most of the actors and cinematographers moved to the Hindi film industry. The Bhojpuri films being produced today are big-budget ones with casts that include top Hindi film actors and actresses. The reason for this change in the taste pattern of Indian movie goers, in spite of the production of a large number of Hindi movies, is that the morals and ethics portrayed in them adhere to the traditional age-old values upheld by the closely knit Indian society, where family and social ties are given immense importance. Hindi movies, on the other hand, are more intent on catering to the tastes of the NRI (non-resident Indian) audiences for whom liberated Western morals and ethics are the order of the day. The middle and upper classes of India have now become disillusioned with the development of the country on the lines of the developed countries of the world through the processes of liberalization and globalization that have strongly eroded the value system of families and consequently of society. These sections now prefer to revert to the traditional values and culture of Indian society as depicted in Bhojpuri films. Thus a powerful shift is visible in the cultural domain of India in favour of Bhojpuri language and culture. This phenomenon is being ameliorated by the considerable Bhojpuri diaspora settled in all parts of the world including the people who migrated from the Bhojpuri region to the Caribbean countries during the colonial period and who have still preserved their Bhojpuri cultural heritage including the Bhojpuri language, albeit in a deviant form because of the influence of myriad languages and cultures over the generations (ibid: 133–134).

## Language of the Hindustani Surinamese

Between 1873 and 1916, the 34,000 indentured labourers from India who went to Suriname took with them several mutually related languages (or dialects) from their home country, among which were Bhojpuri, Magahi and Awadhi. The ensuing interaction among these migrants gave rise to a process that eventually resulted in a new, stabilized language that is not identical to any language in India, and which is called *Sarnami* Hindi, *Sarnami* Hindustani or, simply, *Sarnami*. This language does not seem to be influenced by non-Indic languages, and the early evolution of *Sarnami* was based entirely on an internal process of interaction among the migrants belonging to different language families. The exact number of present-day speakers of *Sarnami* is not known (see 2004 census), but Marhé (1985: 14–15) estimated that in the early 1980s the language was spoken by some 130,000 people in Suriname itself, and by some 100,000 in the Netherlands, whereas around the same time, Sita Kishna (1983: 84) estimated the total number of speakers of *Sarnami*, in both countries together, to be some 180,000 people (Damsteegt 2002: 249).

*Sarnami*, like Bhojpuri in India, was without a high status even for its own speakers, for whom the Indic standard languages Hindi and Urdu, and to some extent Dutch, were prestige languages, although a few scattered novels and poems had been written in *Sarnami* from time to time. In the mid-1970s, a movement arose, primarily among the Hindustanis in the Netherlands, which aimed at generating more respect for *Sarnami* and also at promoting its use in more formal language domains, for example in written fiction and non-fictional texts. It was only with the *Sarnami* movement that the use of the language as a written medium started to spread more widely, and initially considerable results were produced, both in the Netherlands and in Suriname. The movement also stimulated research on the language. It was partly due to these efforts that in 1986 a spelling legislation for writing in the Roman script was passed by the Surinamese government. In fact, texts had already mostly been printed in this script, but occasionally the Indic Hindi alphabet had also been used to arouse the interest of those Hindustanis who were primarily interested in Hindi texts. Though the number of readers must have remained small whatever script was used, the importance of the publications and other activities of the *Sarnami* movement can hardly be overrated (Damsteegt 2002: 251).

Since the beginning of the 1990s, however, hardly any activity has been discernable in the area of *Sarnami*, and the movement does not seem to have had a lasting impact. This does not imply, of course, that *Sarnami* is growing obsolete as a spoken language, on the contrary. However, we do not have any research data to quantify language maintenance. Although members of the other Surinamese groups occasionally learn to speak *Sarnami* in their daily contact with Hindustanis, the language is on the whole an in-group language of the Hindustani ethnic group. In formal situations it is sometimes used in speeches, somewhat hesitantly, alongside the prestige languages. *Sarnami* is hardly ever used in education and has no official status (Damsteegt 2002: 252). It was only with the publication of his poetry in *Sarnami* that the poet Jit Narain placed the *Sarnami* language with a bang on the map for all to hear and thereby giving notice of its presence and talking its rightful place among the other national languages of the land. There is no denying of its beauty, flexibility and liability when skilfully manipulated and moulded by a disciplined craftsman. Jit Narain not only writes *Sarnami* but has also commenced writing poetically the history of a substantial segment of his society and perhaps a segment of Caribbean man in his own language. And to the top of that all his deft use of the only 'Indic' language in the hemisphere has, through his poetic idioms, themes and metaphors, even retained its Puranic' qualities, that is to say that the poet, as all of us, got caught in the ever-present web of memories that even the gods cannot escape from. It is the stories, the histories and the memories, as the poet calls it, of the negative experiences and the hardship of these immigrants and their descendants that he is left with that Jit Narain is mostly and deeply concerned about and that he deals with in his seven books of poetry published so far with Dutch translation overleaf.

Jit Narain (a nom de plume) is a third-generation Hindustani Surinamer who was born in 1948 just outside of then southern limit of

Paramaribo, the capital of Suriname, in a semi-rural and linguistically homogeneous community where he grew up and attended (primary) school before he left Suriname in 1968 for the Netherlands to study medicine (Majumder 2010: 135).

During and upon completion of his medical studies, he settled and practised medicine in The Hague, while promoting the use, valuation and emancipation of *Sarnami*. In 1982 he started, edited and published a magazine, appropriately called *Sarnami*, entirely written in and devoted to the promotion of that language. In fact he practically single-handedly filled this magazine every month – for a period of five years (ibid 135–136).

His first book of poetry, *Dál Bhát Catni* (Yellow Peas, Cooked Rice and Chutney) was published in 1977 in both *Sarnami* – the first-ever literary product in this language – and Dutch. The contract labourers come into focus for the first time in *Sarnami* literature in this collection of poems that are filled with their pain and pathos. Their desperation and disappointment has been described with profound bitterness by Jit Narain. Between 1977 and 2003, six more books of poetry were published, plus a collection of his poetry up to 1988, scripted in Devanagari and published in India. Jit Narain's venture into the *Sarnami* language has encouraged many other modern poets to write in *Sarnami* (ibid).

## *Sarnami* language in the Netherlands

In the Netherlands *Sarnami* is spoken only by two generations of Hindustanis. The third generation understands the language, but many of them are unable to speak it. Many Hindustanis do not even know that their language is called *Sarnami*. They still call it *Sarnami* Hindi or *Sarnami* Hindustani. Neither do they have any knowledge of their mother tongue nor are they interested in learning it. Many Hindustanis are of the opinion that *Sarnami* may not be used outside the kitchen and sitting room as it does not have any prestige. In the mass media like FM radio broadcast and television, the use of *Sarnami* is sporadic.[18] The work of the few *Sarnami* poets and authors who used to write in *Sarnami* is not well-known. Hindustani parents don't even like to speak in *Sarnami* with their children at home since they think that it will affect the performance of the child at school (ibid: 136). This is a situation to be concerned about, because after a few generations, the language will be 'dead' as in Guyana or Trinidad, if nothing is done to turn this trend.

A positive situation is also that young or new politicians also use *Sarnami* in their speeches, along with Dutch and Hindi. There are also pandits and imams/*moulvis* who use *Sarnami* in combination with Hindi/Urdu and even Dutch, because otherwise their message will not reach the audience.

For the Dutch Hindustanis, it is Hindi that has acquired the status of a prestige language and Hindi lessons are given everywhere in the Netherlands through private schools. The reason is the invasion of Bollywood films, film songs and frequent visits to India. Whereas earlier *Sarnami* formed a bridge with Hindi, it now seems to be the other way around (Majumder 2010: 136).

However, there seems to be hope for *Sarnami* language in both Suriname and the Netherlands since in spite of the negative feelings of Hindustanis towards *Sarnami*, a few concerned persons including poets and researchers have been trying hard over the years to make the Hindustanis aware of the richness of the language and revive its lost prestige in their eyes so that the language does not die out altogether. In 2003 a *Sarnami* – Dutch dictionary was compiled, which is an encouraging sign for the future of the language. In addition a new breed of poets has emerged in the Netherlands and Suriname who have started writing exclusively in *Sarnami*, inspired by Jit Narain's *Sarnami* poetry. One such poet is Raj Ramdas, the author of *Kahán hai u* (2003). Along with his book, a CD of the audio recordings of his poem is included, which makes his work accessible to the general public. Raj's poems seldom deal with his background, but his use of *Sarnami* proves how beautiful *Sarnami* can be. Every sentence is a challenge to those who doubted the literary quality of *Sarnami*. Gharietje Choenni's poetry in *Asa* (1980) contains several poems written in *Sarnami*. The young and courageous poet Candani (1965) wrote her first poetry volume *Ghungru tut gail* in 1991 and *Ghar ghar ke khel* (2002). Shrinivasi is another *Sarnami* poet who composed *Buláhat*. However, he never explicitly got involved in the emancipation debates of the *Sarnami* language. Long before he had written and characterized the emotion of Hindustanis as no other poet could do. Chitra Gajadin, another famous *Sarnami* poet, started writing in *Sarnami* after switching over from the Dutch language under the influence of Jit Narain. Apart from expressing their own emotions through their poetry, these poets express the anguish of the Bhojpuris who became *bidesias* during the colonial period and the identity crisis that their future generations are facing because of not being able to come to terms with their present circumstances and who are still unable to answer the question 'who am I' – a Hindustani; a Hindustani from Rotterdam born in Suriname; a Surinamese in the Netherlands or a descendant of ancestors from India, a PIO (person of Indian origin). Hopefully the efforts of these poets will keep the *Sarnami* language alive in both Suriname and the Netherlands so that the history and culture of the *bidesias* are not relegated to the archives of libraries and showcased in museums but remain the living history of their future generations (ibid: 137).

*Some lines from Sarnami poetry*

*Din ke ham kám kari, rát ke dekhi sapná,*
*ájá ke surat láge, thorá-thorá apná.*
*Hamár jahajwá ke nám ná Lálá Rookhwá*
*deswá ke nám bhail Nederland, babuá.*
*K.L.M. se urli ham chorli Sarnamwá*
*yád jab tor áil khoje calli itihaswá*
*Ekar kathá ke ras ná hai pancámritwá*
*kathwá ke kassak kas ke kasle bá mor citwá*
*Káhen u Bhárat choris, ito ham samjhilá*
*Bhárat oke náhi choris, uto ham sahilá*
                              (Jit Narain)
     (From *Agni ke yád/yád ke rákhi* 1991)
                          (Gajadin 2005: 64)

*Translation*

After a hard day's toil we get tired and sleep at night. In our dreams we see our Aja–Aaji (grandfather–grandmother) and we bear a lot of resemblance to each other.

The ship that brought us to the Netherlands was called *Lala Rookh*. Now our homeland is the Netherlands.

First we went to Suriname and then came to the Netherlands via the KLM airlines. After coming here I started recalling my family and set out to search my historical roots.

The tale of coming to the Netherlands from India is not at all interesting; its taste is not like nectar. It is an account of pain that is deeply engraved in our hearts.

I want to understand why my ancestors left India. I understand that my ancestors were not sent forcibly by India, but it was their own choice to leave India. Now we are bearing that pain.

Raj Ramdas's use of *Sarnami* in his poem *Kahán hai u* (2003) proves how beautiful *Sarnami* can be.

*Aj u áwáj káhán*

*jon jiw ke jagái ke*
*dil ke dáná deis kabhi*
*kahán hai u*
*jon berawá khankhanaite*
*khirki kholat rahá*
*andher prán ke*

*kahán hai*
*un tan man ke masti*
*jon jiwan ke khiyáis*
*jawáni ke kaur banáike*
*Kahán*
      (Raj Ramdas)
(From *Kahán hai u* 2003)
   (Gajadin 2005: 63)

*Translation*

Where has that voice got lost today which woke and fed our heart?
Where is he who at the onset of dusk opened windows?
Where is that fun and frolic of our body and mind
which won our heart and instilled in us the aspiration of living?
Where?

  Gharietje Choenni's poetry in *Asa* (1980) contains several poems written in *Sarnami*. She has directness in her writing, which left many (men) flabbergasted after her performances in those years. An example of her style is as follows:

*Bhala batav*
*ka ham bigarli*
*tor re*
*garib bati*
*ohi se ki*
*parhe likhe*
*na janila*
*janta bharmave*
*na janli*
*ki cori chapati*
*na janila*
*baskita bhar*
*larka posila ki*
*dan-dachhina*
*na dei paili*
*ham giral hai*
*tor adhin me*
*ham ghus toke*
*na dei sakli*
  (Gharietje Choenni)
    (from *Asa* 1980)
(Gajadin 2005: 64-65)

*Translation*

Tell us what wrong did I do to you.
We are poor so do not know how to read and write.
We do not know how to baffle people.
We do not know what is robbery and theft.
Anyhow we nurtured and raised our kids.
We could not afford to pay their fees.
We are backward and marginalized only because we did not have any bribe to give.
(The poet here has talked about the poverty and woe faced by people. The reason behind this is the honesty of the Indians.)

*ainá jawáni ke yád kare hai*
*Jindagi katal thokar khát*
*Ab din kate hai aphnái-aphnái*
*behtar yád kisán ke jindagi*
*ab ghari agore hai samay ke*
*ánkhi ban kare khát*
                (Candani)
(from *Ghungru tut gail* 1991)
      (Gajadin 2005: 65–66)

*Translation*

Whenever I look at the mirror I am reminded of my youth days.
Now I am leading a life facing obstacles in my path.
Anyhow I am spending my days and nights huffing and puffing by toiling hard.
The life of a peasant was much better.
Now it is very difficult to spend time.
I am passing my time lying on the cot with my eyes open wide.
(The gist is that a farmer spent all his life toiling hard in the fields. Now during the old days he is just sitting on the cot, and his eyes are waiting for his end time. His heart wants to get quickly rid of his pain.)

*Kaun rátri men hamke boláis hai*
*Aváj báhar se dhire se áil hai*
*Kaun rátri men hamke bolais hai*
*Káheke hamár dvár par áil hai*
*Nautá lekar . . . sáit náu hai*
*Gussáike ke jáne phir laut gail*

*Saramse – álas ham – rah gaily*
*Málum ná hai kaun pukáris*
*Andhiyár men cirág lekar*
*Merhi par se á pukaris*
*Usko jo hamár Bhagván hai.*
*Jabáb deli gadgad dil se*
    (Shrinivasi)
   (from *Anjali* 1963)
   (Gajadin 2005: 66)

*Translation*

Who is calling me in the middle of the night?
A low sound is coming from outside.
I do not know who has called me.
And why he has come at my door.
He has come due to an invitation and not free of cost.
He entered my house and went back angrily.
I did not listen to his voice out of shame.
Who is calling me in the middle of the night?
I lit a lantern in darkness and called him standing on the ridge of the field.
I answered him with a happy heart.
Who is none other than my God!

*Sapná ke gámthi káhe rakhis sáthe*
*Áj aur kál ke khelauná tut jái*
*amdhiyár aur anjor ke málá*
*jápke darvájá*
*khuli bandh hoi*
*khuli bandh hoi*
*hriday ke khirki rahi kháli*
*áw ek bár náple ná gor ke cinhá*
*angná ke dhul toke dur se bolái*
*tor cehrá bhalá kooy pahicani*
*hámth mem anjor leike tu gail rahe*
*dusar desh mem butge hunwá roj*
*tor sapná kharkha pomc leige*
*tor cehrá thakal din hardam*
*yád kare hai sukhal pattá*
*hamár tor bital ádha jiwan andhá*
*ke jáne áj ab sanwer hoi ki ná*

*ab hamlog ke parcháim miti, miti*
*tor angná mem dhire dhire*
            (Chitra Gajadin)
(2007) (Majumder 2010: 143)


*Translation*

Why should I keep the bundle of my dreams with me?
Dreams are our life, if they leave us then our life which is akin to a toy will shatter into pieces.
Dreams are just like the opening and closing of a door.
The window of heart will be left empty when our dreams will not be with us.
If there will be no dreams then how will you recollect the faces of your ancestors?
How will you be associated with the love of your motherland without your dreams?

You went from this land with beautiful dreams and aspirations to an unknown land.
But you had to suffer there.
Your tired face looked just like a dried leaf.
Half of my life has passed with unfulfilled dreams in my heart.
No one knows when we will be able to meet.
(The poetess wants to convey through her poetry that it is dreams that have kept the relationships intact. If we will not dream, then the memory of our homeland will fade from our mind and we will not stay alive. The soil of our earth reminds us of our homeland, our country. An important element of this poem is that it represents the craving of a migrant to meet his family members. He does not know when dawn will approach and he will meet his family.)

## Notes

1  *Khabardar* Part I and II, Wira Production, Wiedjai Rambaram EP (WP 181254).
2  For example R. Bhoelai, Poet Awadh Bihari, Ramsingh Bholasingh, Ramdew Chaitoe, Sahadat Chedi, Bhagavadpersad Hira, Hariparsad Hira, Kees Jagessar, Harridath Jairam, Mehlal Kalpoe, Dew Mangal, Poet Hary Narain, Djagdiesh Oeditram, Kesarie Persad (Djogoe), Satyanand Rekha, Ibrahiem Saddal, Sanatan, Radjoe Sewgolam, Mahendar Sewnandan, Sridath Sewnandan, Dewki Sewlal, Mohammad-Sharief, Poet Wagidhosain and Rakieb Wagidhosain.

3 Some well-known names are Ustad Bahaw Jhinkoe, Hary Goeptar (Mariënburg), Rampersad Ramkhelawan, Poet Ramchander Bansidhar, Ramischander Bihari, Rampersad Bhageloe, Poet Salikram and Hary Sewbalak.
4 To mention some, the family Wagid Hosain (Faziel from THE JUNIORS), family Doelam (Shastri from Indian Temptation), Djwala and Ashni (2Nasty) and DJs like Jairam, 'Prako', 'Hotdog' (Ceicyl), IQ and Jerrel.
5 CD, *doksa ke suruwa*.
6 Much of the drama presented outside Paramaribo remained unnoticed by the Surinamese newspapers. Especially in the western districts, Hindustani drama groups have been particularly active (Van Kempen 2002 IV: 70).
7 Van Kempen apparently mentions this person, as he happens to be the father of the late Prof. Dr Jnan Adhin. Mr Ram Adhin served his contract in British Guyana and came as a free man in 1897 to Suriname. This explains why his name does not occur on the register of immigrants, but on that of foreigners (Nr 611 VR) (Van Kempen IV: 100, n. 496).
8 Raghoebier further mentions several names of authors who at the same time were directors and actors/singers as well: Ramautar Ramkisoen, Soekhlal Gokoel, Ramchander Bansidhar, Ramjattan, Balkisoen Kartaram, Ramsankar, Tamman, Jangabahadur Jodha, Soerjpal, Soeroedjpersad Baldewsingh, Soekhrádj Jagoe (*alias* Chotoe Sankatsingh and zuster Rosa) and Ramcharitar (see also ibid: n. 498). We may further add to this list the names of Doerbalie (Sarmacca) and the currently very popular Gurupersad Baba Niranjan (Rahmalweg).
9 Raghoebier (1987: 87) mentions three other *nautankis*. See further Raghoebier (1987: 87–89), Van Kempen (1987: 125–126) and Bajnath (1979: 19).
10 DWT 5336/8-4-1975. Premiere was in CSS on 3 April 1975.
11 Robby Beerman wrote about this performance that never before had a Hindustani piece of this quality been staged in Suriname (DWT 1210/21-8-1961).
12 Adhin (1998: 115) writes on the importance of this day.
13 In 1971, S.G.M. Kalpoe in the Netherlands wrote a play of the same name.
14 DWT 4601/19-10-1972.
15 DWT 4775/12-4-1973.
16 Gangadien earlier wrote *Baal shaled* (the young Shaled), *Belá ke gawná* (the marriage of Belá) and *Samraat Prithiwiradj tjauhaan* (Emperor Prithiwiradj Tjauhaan).
17 Sahiensa Ramdas in conversation with Maurits Hassankhan, Suriname.
18 The situation is gradually changing. There are several radio stations where the use of *Sarnámi* is stimulated. There are interactive programmes (*opbelprogramma's* = call programmes) where the major language is *Sarnámi*.

# 5

# STILL THEY ARE MIGRATING

## Contemporary migration from Bhojpuri region

*Piya Mor Gailan Pardes, ae Batohi Bhaiya*
*Raat Naahi Neend Din Tani Na Chainwa, ae batohi bhaiya*
(Bhikhari Thakur)
(Yadav and Singh (ed.) 2005: 39)

(My husband has gone to a distant land, O passerby
I have sleepless nights and restless days, O passerby)

*Bhaiya Express* is the name of a short story written by Arun Prakash about the migration of labourers, who are also called *bhaiya* (brother) in the place where they migrate. In this chapter we take '*bhaiya* express' as the metaphor for trains that convey migrants. In colonial times the trains took them to depots from where they were taken overseas by ship. Today the trains carry migrants from villages like Semra, Barwaripur and Majhauwa to cities like Delhi, Mumbai, Calcutta, Surat or those in Assam and Punjab, where they work as labourers or from where they travel further by aeroplane. The places from where these people migrate are Azamgarh, Ghazipur, Basti, Banda, Gorakhpur, Sultanpur, Gonda, Faizabad and so on in the eastern part of Uttar Pradesh and Raxaul, Narkatiaganj, Betia, Sugauli, Motihari, Chakia, Darbhanga, Madhubani, Jaynagar, Nirmali, Farbisganj, Munger, Purnea, Saharsa, Begusarai, Araria, Sitamarhi, Vaishali, Chhapara, Gopalganj, Bhojpur, Buxar and so on in Bihar. Each day at least a hundred people gather at the railway station or bus depot in these places and reach the closest railway junction like Allahabad, Banaras, Katihar, Barauni, Samastipur, Mokama, Patna, Buxar, Ara, Sasaram, Muzaffarpur, Chhapra and Siwan, which lie on the route of long-distance trains. Most of these people are not aware of their destination or the direction in which it lies. They are under the complete custody and protection of the labour contractors who beg or cajole, lure or threaten them to go to work in factories in big cities where labour is needed. These labour contractors are like modern-day recruiters or *arkatiyas* of the colonial times who travelled from village to village and influenced hapless innocent people to work as '*girmitia* labourers' in colonial overseas plantations (Majumder 2010: 59–60).

Migration from these places is at its peak between April and July and between October and January. During these months all day and night, there is a great deal of commotion at the railway stations. The migrants, with their bundles containing wheat bread (*roti*), powdered pulse (*sattu*), flat rice (*chiwra*) and savouries (*thekua*), a water container and a small bundle of clothes, wait on the platforms for the trains. Each group has a leader who knows from where the migrants have been brought, where they are going, which train they have to catch, in which train they will be fined if they travel and other minute details about the journey. The duration for which a train stops is very less, so the leader has to hustle the people in his group into an unreserved general compartment, making sure that no one is left behind (ibid: 60).

When trains like Sealdah Express, Vaishali Express, Shaheed Express, Amrapali Express, Howrah Mail and Muzaffarpur–Amritsar Express enter into the platform, all the migrants rush into them. The tremendous crowd inside the general compartments often forces the migrants to travel on the roofs of the compartment. During the peak migration seasons, as the trains move into Bihar and East Uttar Pradesh, the crowd on top of the general compartments becomes larger and larger. Forget about lying down, there is no place even to sit or breathe properly. The agonizing journey on the roofs of the compartment that is fraught with mortal danger cannot be expressed in mere words. Sometimes when the diesel engines of the trains are changed with electric engines, the passengers are made to get off the roofs, sometimes at midnight in the middle of nowhere. Without any idea about their whereabouts or the name of their destination points, one can only imagine the plight of the hapless migrants. Often it happens when the train passes through a station with a low ceiling or where the height of the signal is low. If a migrant happens to doze off, he will hit his head against signal and fall right off the train, either dying immediately or injuring himself permanently. The rest of the people on the roof will not even know what happened to their co-passenger. The number of persons who disappear in this manner is a grim testimony to the plight of people who are forced by their economic conditions to leave the secure haven of their villages and travel to unknown places under inhuman conditions. The passengers who survive the journey travel under pitiable conditions of burning heat, shivering cold or heavy rains with only a thin cloth over their bodies to cover them. Neither do they have enough clothes to protect themselves nor are their bodies strong enough to withstand the forbidding weather conditions. Somehow or the other they manage to reach their destination points where the future awaiting them is far grimmer and bleaker than their journey (ibid: 60–61).

During the colonial period Calcutta was the most important destination point for migrants from where they were shipped overseas. Today Punjab has emerged as the single largest destination point of migrants from Bihar and Uttar Pradesh. Apart from Punjab, some labourers also migrate to Delhi, Calcutta, Assam, Mumbai, Surat and other big places in India, and to Dubai, Saudi Arabia and so on outside India. In Punjab there is a tremendous demand for labourers to work in the big farms in rural areas and in the factories in cities like Ludhiana, Amritsar and Jalandhar. As soon as the trains enter Punjab, at each station the labourers are greeted by armies of farmers seated in trailers and tractors. The agents of owners of factories located in the cities and *munims*, who are the recruiters of *mandi ke arhti* (another link in the chain of recruiters), are also present. Bidding for the labourers begins at the stations themselves. Sometimes this auction begins at the Ambala–Saharanpur station, which is right on the border of Punjab. Broadly two kinds of labourers are recruited for working in this state. One category is the farm labourers who are skilled in farm work like sowing, ploughing, harvesting and sieving. The demand for this labour is seasonal, depending on the agricultural season. The labourers work in Punjab during the cultivation seasons and then go back to their native villages. But the amount they earn in these seasons is much higher than that earned by the other category of labourers, namely the unskilled factory workers. The skilled farm labourers are in greater demand than the unskilled factory labourers since the entire economy of Punjab, which is mainly based on agriculture, depends upon them. Around fifteen years ago when the terrorist movement was on in Punjab, farm labourers were recruited from their native villages by labour contractors who were hired by farmers for this purpose. The method of recruiting them was luring them with tempting offers to go to Punjab since no one was readily willing to go there. If that did not work, they were openly threatened to go. Often the farmers themselves went all the way to Darbhanga, Madhubani, Katihar, Azamgarh, Sultanpur, Allahabad and so on and roped in labourers by paying them large advance amounts. These methods of recruitment are very similar to those used during the colonial period to recruit indentured labourers to work in overseas plantations. Today there is no need for the farmers to go to the villages or to employ labour contractors, since the labourers themselves go to Punjab in search of work (ibid: 61–62).

Often it happens that the labourers who work a few seasons with a particular farmer develop a good relationship with him. During off seasons when they go back to their villages they even exchange letters with the farmer. Every year they go back to the same farmer in the expectation of being hired. It is only when the farmer tells them that there is no work do they allow themselves to be hired by other farmers or contractors. The farm labourers working and living in big farms enjoy a comparatively better situation than the factory workers living in big cities. Although the living quarters of the farm workers are small, they get food, fresh air, adequate water supply, good sleep at night since they do not need to work in shift duties and, most importantly, respect from the farmers and their families with whom they develop a good relationship since they often become permanent workers on the farms. On the other hand, the unskilled factory workers live in highly inhuman conditions. There is no shortage of work for them since there is always a dearth of labourers in factories. If they like, they can earn a good amount of money by working long hours, spending a small sum on food and living with a large number of labourers so that the rent per head is reduced. The demand for living space for labourers in cities has caused the springing up of high-rise buildings called *barha* that strongly resemble hencoops in which hens are stuffed without mercy. The rooms are constructed in two rows on either side of a tiny courtyard, measuring seven by seven feet. The number of rooms in quarters such as these varies, but some of these quarters contain nearly 108 rooms while some contain as many as 422 rooms. For each twelve rooms, there is a handpump and a toilet. These *barhas* are very similar to the quarters in which the migrants were made to live when they reached Suriname to work as indentured labourers during the colonial period (ibid: 62–63).

Each of these rooms houses seven to eight labourers. The neighbourhood grocery shop owner or ration shop owner acts as the contact person between the labourers and the owners of these quarters. The owners pass on the responsibility of collecting rent from the labourers to them, while they themselves live in big houses in posh areas of the city. Each room is let out to three or four persons who share the rent, but usually the labourers stuff in around seven to eight persons so that the rent per head is decreased. But the small size of the room forces them all to sleep on the floor since it will not be possible to accommodate so many cots in the room. The floors of the rooms are covered with mats, dhurries, bed sheets and other kinds of materials to spread on the floor for sleeping. Sometimes in summer a few even sleep on the terrace (ibid: 63).

Most of the money earned by the labourers is saved by them to send back home. They themselves live extremely frugally, striving to survive on two sets of clothes, a small amount of food and only the bare minimum needs. Almost all the migrants live in quarters such as these in the cities to where they migrate. But the survey of the *bidesia* villages shows that the amount that they bring back from their stay is grossly inadequate to compensate for the long period of separation and the suffering experienced by the family members. The *Nishads* of Barwaripur, who are skilled fishermen, go to Mumbai to catch fish on a contract of eight months, at the end of which they are paid Rs 25,000 in cash. The unskilled *Chamars* and other Dalits who go to Delhi or Mumbai bring back a saving of only Rs 10,000 after eight months. The *Nishads*, however, are facing stiff competition from fishermen of other castes, which is making them sceptical of getting the same amount in the next season. The reduction in the signing amount, however, is not a deterrent for them since the poverty in the villages where they live is so acute that they desperately need even a small amount of additional money for their family members to survive (ibid).

## Half there, half here: narratives of separation

There are many remote villages in Uttar Pradesh and Bihar that saw the migration of able-bodied men to foreign lands during the colonial period. This tradition is still continuing, and even today migration of males from villages of this region to other places inside India is the rule rather than the exception. See figure 5.1.

For an understanding of the Bhojpuri culture in general, we did a survey of the villages that lie in the Bhojpuri region of India. A review study of the literature on Bhojpuri culture by Upadhyaya (1999), Singh (2001), and Indra Deva (1989) provided us a background for our study. We also gained information about the various folk forms like *kajri, jantsar* and *birha* and the places where these are still in practice. We collected CDs, folk songs and videos and on the basis of these materials tracked the Bhojpuri regions from where most of migration had occurred and is still occurring. This helped us in the selection of the villages for our study.

On the basis of the secondary information and the material collected, we selected the villages Barwaripur (see figure 5.2), Semra and Majhauwa for our study. The villages selected were such places from where migration had taken place in the colonial period and which are also the site of contemporary migration. These villages are culturally vibrant, and popular culture, folk culture, is still alive in these villages. The *bidesia* culture is vibrant even today in these villages.

A large number of men have migrated from these villages to work in various cities of India like Surat, Delhi, Ghaziabad and Mumbai. As a result, these villages are filled with women whose husbands are away in *pardes* and they are running their households single-handedly. From

*Figure 5.1* Migrants Outside a Station Waiting for Their Trains to Go to Their Destination. Photograph: Brijendra Gautam, December 2014

the villages like Semra and Majhauwa, men have migrated to cities like Meerut and Delhi for a better livelihood.

In this section we will document the life stories of women like Geeta Nishad, Anara, Savitri Devi, Rita and Indrawati of the aforementioned villages whose husbands are away in *pardes*. We will also document the pain and suffering of the men of these villages who have migrated to other cities for a living and left their near and dear ones behind.

## Narratives of women

### Geeta Nishad, Barwaripur[1]

My name is Geeta Nishad, and I live in Barwaripur village. I have five children, and my husband is a migrant who goes for eight months every year to Mumbai to work as a fisherman. I came to this village nearly fifteen years ago after my marriage, with dreams in my heart like every new bride has. My new family was very small. There was only my father-in-law, my mother-in-law, my brother-in-law and my sister-in-law, apart from the two of us. The day-to-day needs of our family were somehow being fulfilled. My father-in-law did not own any land but sustained the family by doing small-time menial labour work wherever he could find it in the village. There was only one earning member and five stomachs to fill. How long could this situation continue? Nearly every day there were quarrels between my husband and his father. My husband wanted to leave the village to search for work, but my father-in-law wanted him to work inside the village. My husband felt that working in the village meant losing his honour since he would be working as someone's servant. Besides the work should be such that he could get a good amount of money in return for his hard labour. In the village there was no scope of work except working in the fields of the *Thakurs*. The daily wage rate in the village was very low, and in addition he would also have to suffer the ill-treatment of the *Thakurs*. All these considerations made my husband decide against working in the village (Majumder 2010: 66–67).

These constant quarrels made me very anxious about the future. I could not get rid of the haunting fear that I would soon be separated from my husband. At that time many women of our community told me that their husbands were leaving the village for *pardes* in search of jobs. I did not tell my husband about it for fear that he too would leave. But this was a foolish thought since such facts are not hidden for long. Finally what I was scared about happened. I heard the news from people that my husband was leaving for Mumbai along with other men of the village. I also understood that they would have to stay there for eight months at a stretch. The malik stopped work for four months when the labourers were given leave to go home (ibid: 67).

The very thought of separating from my husband made my blood run cold. All kinds of thoughts kept running through my mind. I made up all kinds of excuses to prevent him from going. But there was no way to stop him. He had made up his mind to go. To make him understand my feelings better, I sang the following song to him:

> *Piya mat jaa bideshwa rahab kaise*
> *Piya mat jaa bideshwa rahab kaise*
> *Sasura ke batiya to sahi sun lebe*
> *Sasura ke batiya to sahi sun lebe*
> *Saas ke boliya sahib kaise*
> *Piya mat ja bideshwa rahab kaise*
> *Piya mat ja bideshwa rahab kaise*
> *Dewra ke batiya to sahi sunlebe*
> *Dewra ke batiya to sahi sunlebe*
> *Nanadiya ke boliya sahib kaise*

*Piya mat ja bideshwa rahab kaise*
*Piya mat ja bideshwa rahab kaise*

Translation

O my husband don't go to Bides, how will I live.
O my husband don't go to Bides, how will I live.
My father-in-law's words I can stand.
My father-in-law's words I can stand.
But my mother-in-law's words how will I stand.
O my husband don't go to Bides how will I live.
My brother-in-law's words I can stand.
My brother-in-law's words I can stand.
But my sister-in-law's words how will I stand.
O my husband don't go to Bides how will I live.
O my husband don't go to Bides how will I live. (ibid: 67–68)

Geeta lamented that her pathos-ridden song also did not have any effect on her husband. She continued, 'The need of the house and the family members was money, which could be met only by leaving the village. The preparations for his departure began in early *Magh* (January). Soon the time came for him to leave. He took a local train from Sultanpur to Allahabad junction, and from there he caught a train to Mumbai. For two or three days after the departure of my husband, his family members wept for him but then they went back to their own routine lives. But I was the one who had to bear the pain at his leaving. My heart was filled with grief, but I had to put up a brave front'. (ibid: 68)

(Here Geeta sang another song to express the feelings of a deserted wife in the different seasons and months of the year.)

*Birahin tarhpe sejaria majhare man mare*
*Baisakhwa ke kai gaye karare sejariya majhare*
*Jeth maas ati dhoop parat hai*
*Choli dharat nisare*
*Laage asharh gagan dhan garjat*
*Saawan uthe baadal kare sejariya majhare*
*Bhadon mein ati megh parisai*
*Bharigaye taal talare*
*Kwar maas swami ghar aavat*
*Kaatik laage ratiya piyari sejariya majhare*
*Agahan maas ati jaarh parat hai*
*Choli chadar tane sejariya majhare*

*Sitaram poos jab laagat*
*Piya maghwa mein aai gaye duare*
*Sejariya majhare*


*Translation*

A deserted wife is suffering in the middle of the bed.
My husband promised to come in *Baisakh* (spring).
In the hot month of *Jeth*
my tight blouse torments me.
When it is the month of *Asharh* thunder rumbles in the sky.
And as black clouds rain heavily, I suffer in the middle of the bed.
In the month of *Magh* rain clouds cover the sky.
And all the lakes and ponds fill with water.
In the month of *Kunwar* my husband comes home.
The nights are wonderful in the month of *Kartik* in the middle of the bed.
In the biting cold during the month of *Agahan*
I cover my blouse with a sheet in the middle of the bed.
Sitaram (the poet) says that after the month of *Poos*
when the month of *Magh* arrives
my husband stands at the doorstep
in the middle of the bed. (ibid: 68–69)

As the days went rolling by, I had to control my sorrow and work extra hard since I had to do single-handedly all the work that my husband did earlier. Life in the village is extremely hard, and each season brings a new hardship with it. In winter, when cold winds blow and we are too poor to buy enough warm clothes to protect ourselves, I have to go alone to collect firewood to keep the house warm and also to cook food for my children and the other members of the family. In summer, we poor people have to face a different kind of hardship when the hot sun blazes down and scorches us all. Without a fan in the house we can't even sit inside to cool ourselves while it is impossible to sit outside, with the hot winds blowing continuously. Even in the heat I have to go and collect firewood to cook food for everyone. The worst season is the rainy season when there are huge puddles all around and the thatch straw roof on our mud house cannot provide enough protection from the rain. Just before the rainy season, I have to cover the roof with plastic sheets to make sure that water does not seep through the gaps in the roof. All these household activities had to be performed by me, with no one to help in the absence of my husband. I had to also prepare fodder for the cattle

*Figure 5.2* Women in Barwaripur Village, Sultanpur District, Uttar Pradesh, Sharing Their Folk Forms. Photograph: Brijendra Gautam, December 2014

and send them out for grazing. In addition, I had to earn money for the daily needs of the house by twining rope, which I sold in the *haat* (local market) everyday (ibid: 69).

Without enough words to express her difficulties, Geeta sang another folk song narrating the hardships that a migrant's wife has to face in different seasons.

The first time when he went, it was worse for me because it was the first time when I had been separated from him. Somehow I passed the days one by one. I had to bear the exploitation of my father-in-law, mother-in-law, sister-in-law and brother-in-law who took advantage of my husband's absence to make me work like a servant in the house. I worked throughout the day without a second's rest. No one was there to consider my feelings as a new bride. My sorrow, my pain and my sufferings without my husband cannot be expressed in words. My husband also did not think of my feelings since he did not bother to send me even a single letter in all the eight months he was away, which I could read and console myself. At night I lied tossing and turning in my bed, praying to God for my husband's well-being and to send him back to me soon.

I understood that it was essential for him to leave me and the village to earn money, but my heart refused to be pacified (ibid: 69–70).

Somehow the eight months passed, and soon it was time for him to return. One by one the men of the village who had also gone to Mumbai started returning. From these men I understood that my husband too would be coming back soon. The village had already started getting a festive look, with each household from where men had gone to *pardes* brimming with laughter and joy. All the women who had been waiting eagerly for their husbands felt their patience had been justified. Each one's husband had brought new clothes and gifts for them and their children, which they proudly showed to the other women. My husband was one of the last to return, and I waited impatiently for him to come back (ibid: 70).

Soon one day my impatience ended. It was time for my husband to arrive. I got up early in the morning to clean the house with cow dung. Then I took my bath and started preparing different kinds of food items to welcome my husband. I then wore a bright saree, put on whatever little ornaments I had and waited for him. When I saw my *pardesi* husband finally walking towards the house, my heart leaped up in joy. After greeting all his family members, my husband finally greeted me. But I did not show him how happy I was since I wanted to punish him for making me suffer for so many months. I did not respond to his greeting but gave him a piece of gur (jaggery, unrefined sugar) with a serious face and then turned away. But later, as soon as he touched me, my anger melted like wax and I felt that I was the happiest woman on the earth (ibid).

The first time my husband had brought Rs 8,000 as savings from his earnings in Mumbai. He had also brought new clothes for everyone in the house and a saree and a pair of earrings for me. The entire money was spent in buying cereals and pulses to last the whole year, repairing the house, buying a few extra sets of clothes for the family and repaying some of the outstanding debts that I had accumulated when I was short of money. My husband spent the first month after his return in eating, sleeping, relaxing and doing odd jobs in the house. The next three months he spent in working as a daily labourer in the village to earn some money for the house. Somehow the four months went off, and soon it was time for him to leave again for Mumbai. Last time when he went I was a new bride and did not have the courage to talk to him freely. This time I broke my earlier shyness and made him promise that he would write to me (ibid: 70–71).

After four months of happiness, once again the clouds of sorrow gathered around me. But this time I was waiting for my baby to be born.

A few days after his departure my first child was born. I was happy to become a mother but sad because my husband was not there to share my happiness. This time his absence hit me harder because I had to do all the household activities in addition to looking after the baby. For a few days I wept for my husband, but soon I dried my eyes and drowned myself in work. Thankfully after a few months, his letter arrived, giving his address where he was living in Mumbai. Since I was a little literate and could read and write, I wrote to him that he had become a father. He came to know about the birth of his child three months after the birth (ibid: 71).

Today I am the mother of five children. Now his arrival and departure has become a routine thing in my life. But now in addition to worrying about my husband's living in *pardes*, I also have to worry about the upbringing of my children single-handedly with no one to share the trials and tribulations of their growing up. Earlier when my family was small, the savings that my husband brought from Mumbai seemed a large amount. But now that we have a large family to support this amount is barely adequate. Another thing that has affected us adversely is that now the competition for work with the contractor in Mumbai has greatly increased. More and more people from our village and other adjoining villages are desperately seeking work there. Since the supply of workers is greatly exceeding the demand, the contractors have decreased the contract amount. For the last few years my husband is being paid only Rs 5,000 as the contract amount for eight months, out of which he is able to save only Rs 3,500. This amount is too small to sustain such a large family for the whole year. So I have to supplement it by twining more and more ropes to sell in the market. After completing all my household activities, in the afternoon I sit down to coil two to four kilograms of rope, for which I get between Rs 10 and 20. With this amount I am able to buy vegetables and cereals for the evening meal (ibid).

One thing that is helping to comfort me is that with the spread of communication technology in villages, I am in direct touch with my husband over phone. On the last day of every month he rings up at a fixed time at the Bania's (grocer) shop where I wait to receive his phone call. I now feel less distant from him since I can hear his voice and we can share each other's problems. The distance from our village to *pardes* now does not seem so far any more. Letters do not serve the same purpose since they take a long time to reach and often get lost in transit. Also the news becomes stale by the time it reaches its destination. This is the story of my life – the story of a wife whose husband is in *pardes* and who is suffering silently waiting for her husband to return with the money that will compensate for this suffering (ibid: 72).

## Anara, Barwaripur[2]

Another woman of Barwaripur village is Anara whose husband Om Prakash has been away working in different places for many years. She narrated the story of her trials and tribulations and her joy and sorrows in the following words.

My natal house is in Jaunpur. I got married at a very early age and my *gauna* (ceremony that takes place after the bride attains puberty when she is send off to her husband's house) took place after nine years. In those nine years I had no conversation with my husband, but after going to his house we used to take each other's *haal-khabar* (asking after one's well-being). A few months after my *gauna*, my husband went to *pardes*. At that time I was in my natal home. A few months later he came to visit me. At my parent's house, I could not talk much with him so could not request him not to go but the next time when he returned I was at my in-law's house. Then I begged him not to go by telling him that we would manage on whatever little we have here, but my husband did not heed my words. Now he has been living away for the past seventeen or eighteen years, and I have become used to his absence.

It is difficult to narrate in a few words the condition of a woman whose husband is away. My heart felt that it would burst the first time when he went. The first few days I consoled myself by chanting in my mind over and over again that he has gone to *pardes* because he needs to earn money. He has a large extended family to support. He could not have managed by living in the village, so he had to go. By repeating these lines to myself, I gradually overcame my sorrow. The next time when he came, I requested him to take me with him. Since I had no children, he took me to Assam, Kanpur, Delhi and so on, wherever he found work. Now that we have children, it is not possible for him to take all of us with him.

My husband's absence has made me the butt of taunts, jokes and jeers of all the women of my *basti*. When they joke with me, I also joke back, but when they taunt me I feel very sad. Earlier there was no facility for telephoning, so I could not communicate with him. Being illiterate, I could not write myself; neither could I ask someone else to write letters for me since I was afraid they would fall into the hands of the elders of my house. Sometimes when he wrote letters, I would get them read by my younger sister-in-law. I would also ask her to write my *haal-khabar* and that of the children. Sometimes I would ask her to write *Dohas* (couplets) or *Sher-o-Shairi* (love poems in Urdu). I would send them through the hands of a very reliable courier without the knowledge of my own parents or his parents. Now he rings up once in a while so we can talk each other's *haal-khabar* directly.

My husband works as a welder in Delhi. He joins scooter parts, makes nets and so on. Here we have around one bigha land, which is too small to sustain our big family. Only a small amount of cereals and vegetables grow in it. There is no work available in our village to supplement the output from the land. My husband's earnings from his stay in *pardes* help us to fulfil our requirements. We are able to send our children to school only because of his earnings and savings. Earlier when we lived together in a joint family, the money was sent to my mother-in-law. Now that our household has separated, the money comes in my name, but I also have to do single-handedly what my husband would have done had he been here. I have to cook food, clean the house, feed the children, wash the clothes and alongside tend the cattle, which is a big job. In my spare time I weave baskets to fill my loneliness. Sometimes when my sisters-in-law come over for a visit, we discuss our husbands and share our joys and sorrows.

When my husband comes, he usually stays for around fifteen days. Sometimes he even stays for two months at a stretch. During that period, the whole environment of our house changes. When he comes, I release all the sorrows, the misery and the sufferings that I keep bottled up inside me during his absence. I quarrel with him the whole day long, but later on we make up. He also asks me the news about all the people of our family. I the whole day spend in a daze, making special food items for him and ensuring that he has a pleasant stay. When he leaves again, I feel very sad. I would like to see him off at the bus station when he leaves, but he forbids me from doing so since he feels sad when he sees my sorrowful face. After leaving the house, he does not look back; otherwise he will suffer in *pardes*.

I have become very superstitious about my husband since his departure. There are many superstitions that the people of this village believe and that I too have started believing. It is believed that when a bird called *shuklain* calls, the husband will come bearing money and gifts. When a green spider climbs up one's left shoulder, then the husband will bring items for makeup (*shauk-shringaar ke samaan*). A black spider does not specify anything special. If a woman's left palm itches, it is a good omen, while the itching of the right palm is a bad omen. If a woman dreams of small fishes or of a snake striking someone, it is a good sign. All the women of this village whose husbands are away take these dreams and superstitions very seriously since they are all worried about the well-being of their husbands and would like them to return soon bearing gifts for them.

In the absence of my husband, I feel very lonely. All the worries of my house are on my shoulders. To escape from these anxieties, I sing *bidesia* songs and dance with the other women of the *basti*.

### *Savitridevi, Semra*[3]

I came to village Semra with my husband Balji long ago, but I did not get the pleasure of living with him. After a few months of my marriage, my husband got a government job in Meerut. I was very thankful to God for granting him this offer for which he had been waiting for a long time, but I was also sorrowful at the thought of separating from him when he left for Meerut. At the time of his departure, however, I did not reveal my sorrow but sent him off happily. This was the beginning of an unending chain of arrivals and departures by him when he used to come to our village for short visits every few months. In the meantime I gave birth to four children, two daughters and two sons. Looking after them took all my time, which helped me to overcome the sorrow of my husband's absence. We own a large tract of land, and I also have to look after it. My children are too small to help me although they run small errands for me.

Earlier I passed my days waiting for my husband's letters to come. I got them read by my sons since I myself am illiterate. In reply I would inform him about all that was happening in the village, including news about the land and the children. I wrote about everything except my pain and how I was surviving without him. I know that he too suffers a great deal without us, so much so that once, a few years ago, he fell badly ill in Meerut. One of his colleagues rang me up at a neighbour's house to inform me. The news was a great shock to me. I became desperate to go to him and tend him in his illness. Immediately I made arrangements to leave my children with my sister-in-law who stays in the same village and boarded the next train to Meerut.

The sight of him lying ill on a cot made my heart grow cold. I stayed with him for four months and helped him to recuperate from his illness. When he had recovered completely, I decided it was time to turn my attention to my children and go back to the village. It was very heart-rending to leave him behind, but I had no other option. Being a mother I also had to take care of my children, so it was a compulsion for me to return. I knew it would be extremely painful for me, worrying about my husband on one hand and the children on the other and managing all the household affairs on my own. In addition I had to feed the cattle, plough the fields, sow the seeds, reap the harvest and do the numerous other things that need to be done on a farmland. I did all the work, but my mind was always on my husband and his welfare. Thankfully he had started making phone calls to the village at an interval of fifteen to twenty days at the grocer's shop in the market. Being in the market I could not always go to receive the phone calls, but my sons used to go.

Everything was going on well, but suddenly one day my eldest daughter fell seriously ill. I ran and fetched a doctor, but he suggested hospitalization. Not having enough money, I rang up my husband and asked him to come immediately with the money. He said he would come but added that he would have to wait till his leave was sanctioned, which would take a few days. I went back home in a terrible state of mind to tend to my daughter, whose condition was getting worse. On the fourth day, she expired without seeing her father. He came to the village a few days later with the money to hospitalize her, but it was used instead for her last rites.

Since that time I have lost all interest in life. Now I do not care whether he is here or not. I will look after his fields and his children till my last breath since it is my duty, but now his presence or absence is immaterial to me. I know my husband is also not happy at his place of work, but he has to stay there to earn money to sustain our family. It is our poverty that has forced my husband to go to *pardes* and my daughter to *parlok* (nether world). What kind of life is this? Neither my husband is happy, nor are we happy here. But somehow we have to survive till we die.

### *Rita, Majhauwa*[4]

My name is Rita, and I am twenty-six years old. My husband's name is Ramashish, and he is thirty years old. I have been living in this village for the past six years. I live with my mother-in-law, father-in-law, brother-in-law and sister-in-law since my husband is in Delhi. He had been living away from his house for many years before my marriage. After my marriage I came to know that earlier he worked at making iron chains in this village, but later he became dissatisfied and left for Delhi with a few other boys of this village. After leaving the village, he did not come back for four years. Nor did he send any message home. Four years later when he returned, he informed his family members that he is working in a factory where he makes things with plaster of Paris.

We got married when my husband came home from Delhi once. But he went back alone only fifteen days after the marriage. Earlier, before our marriage he did not send any money to his parents, but after our marriage he started sending money for my upkeep. I do not know how much money he earns there or how much he saves, but I know that he is satisfied with his work there and does not want to return to the village. At the time of my marriage I knew that I would not be able to live permanently with my husband. But I had decided that I would be satisfied with whatever little time I got to spend with him. I am not happy here without him, but I know that he too is not happy without me. The living conditions there are very bad since five men have to share one room.

After working hard the whole day, he has to come back home and cook his own food. In spite of having a wife, he has to live like this, the reason being poverty and the absence of job opportunities in the village.

Sometimes I wish I could muster the courage to tell him to take me with him, but I know that he cannot afford to hire a separate house for me there. We own one bigha land in the village, and we grow a few crops, which help to sustain our family. My husband's absence hits me dearly all the time, but in spite of my heartfelt desire, I cannot live with him. It is six years since I got married, but I still do not have any children. Sometimes I wonder whom I am living for, but then I console myself with the thought that my husband loves and cares for me, although we cannot live together. Now my husband comes home every six months for a few days. I miss him the most on festive occasions when all the ladies dress up nicely and proudly go out with their husbands. Thankfully we can talk often over the phone, which helps to reduce the pain of separation. I keep waiting for his phone calls to come so that I can release my sadness and grief at his absence. Before coming, he always asks me what he should bring for me. I reply that I would be happy with a saree or an ornament, but I know that my real happiness would be when I set my eyes on him.

### *Indrawati, Majhauwa*[5]

My name is Indrawati, and I am forty-two years old. I have been living in the Harijan Basti of Majhauwa for the past twenty-five years. One year after my marriage, my husband went to Calcutta in search of a job. His aunt lived in Govindpur near Calcutta, where she and her husband had a big business selling flowers, fruits, vegetables and so on. Even after three years of hunting for a job when he could not find one, she employed him to transport milk to and from Calcutta. In those three years, he did not visit the village even once. I constantly prayed to God to help him get a good job. Thankfully He heard my prayers, and my husband found employment as a cashier in Allahabad Bank.

Six months after he joined, he visited the village for a week. I was in the seventh heaven of delight when he arrived. I felt that my God had come. I could not get enough of him. After he left, I was once again drowned in sorrow. My father-in-law, mother-in-law and brother-in-law lived with me, and I was responsible for looking after them. This kept me busy, but I was sad because I could not live with him. I think my husband too felt the same because after one year when he returned he asked me to accompany him. Initially this caused a lot of tension in our house because my in-laws did not want me to go, but since my brother-in-law had got married one year earlier and his wife was there to look after everyone, they reluctantly agreed. So I went with my husband to Calcutta.

We rented a small house in Calcutta, and there I began my first household. I gave birth to two children there. For the first two years, everything went well. But gradually as the children started growing older, our troubles started. My husband's job was transferable, and he was frequently posted to remote areas. It was getting difficult to ensure a good education for the children since they too had to change schools frequently. It was also too expensive for me to stay behind in Calcutta with the children while my husband set up a separate establishment at his place of transfer. On the other side my brother-in-law and his family had separated from our joint family and there was no one to look after my in-laws. So I took the decision to go back to the village with the children twelve years after living with my husband.

After returning to the village, my life became extremely busy. I had to single-handedly admit my children in school, feed the cattle, milk the cows every morning and evening, look after my in-laws and children, take them to the doctor when they fell ill and also do all the household work. Sometimes I wished that my husband was with me to share my burden, but it was not possible for him to leave his permanent and stable job. He wrote to me once every month, and I waited impatiently for his letters throughout the month. I saved his old letters to read them over and over again. I never wrote to him because I was worried that the person whom I sent to post the letters would open and read them.

Slowly, as the children started going to higher classes, the money that my husband used to send became insufficient for our needs, so every month he started sending a little more by saving from his needs there. Earlier he sent the money by money order for which I went to Jokahra post office and waited for hours there. When I conveyed my problem to my husband, he helped me to open a joint account and started sending the money by bank draft. As time passed and our village became connected with modern technology, his letters started decreasing and he started making phone calls more frequently. It was euphoric to hear his voice on the phone so often. I felt that he was very close to me, and the distance from the village to Calcutta seemed very little.

Today it is twenty-two years since he has been living in *pardes*. Now that the children have grown older, I can visit him once in a while. I cannot stay away from the house for very long, so I usually go for only a month or two. But as our ages are advancing and our body strength is decreasing, we have both started realizing that it is important for us to stay together at this age. When he comes to the village every six months, he feels very upset at the time of going back. I also feel extremely sad. Today

I have everything that I want for a comfortable living, but I am deprived from the most important thing for a woman, which is to look after her husband. After my husband leaves, for two or three days I cry but then I go back to my work routine. Now that my daughter is old enough to get married, I pray to God that she lives with her husband and does not experience the same sufferings that I did throughout my life.

## Narratives of men

### Chhotu, Semra[6]

My name is Chhotu. I live in Semra village. I went to Surat at the age of twenty-two years. My cousin had been working there for the past ten years, and he asked me to join him. I would not have gone to Surat had not our family's condition been so poor. In my childhood my father worked as a truck driver. Today his health has broken down, and he can no longer drive a truck. The tiny amount of land that our family owned was too inadequate to sustain our big family. There is also no scope for seeking employment elsewhere. All these reasons led me to decide to migrate to Surat.

I asked my mother, 'Amma, should I go or not?' Amma replied, 'It is your wish. You can go if you like.' So I left my house and went to Surat. I took a tempo from my house to Allahabad, and from there I caught a bus for Mirzapur. At Mirzapur I boarded the Ganga Tapti Express, which goes straight to Surat. Although Surat was an unknown city for me, my cousin had given me detailed directions, so I reached the office of the *Pandor* society to meet Lakkhichand and ask him for a job. Since my cousin had had initial discussions regarding me, I joined work the very next day.

I got Rs 80 as daily wages every day at my workplace. So in one month, I earned Rs 2,400. Out of this, I paid Rs 700 as rent for my room each month. Before renting the room, I had to pay Rs 500 to the landlord as security, which I later got back. After buying the essential commodities, I could manage to save only Rs 500 each month. I sent this sum back home. Today my salary has increased to Rs 2,700, out of which I spend Rs 1,500 on my necessities. I save the rest of the amount, that is Rs 1,200, and send it home from time to time. I am unable to buy anything out of this for me, my wife or my children and parents. I buy my shirts when I go back to my village and wear them throughout the year.

I work very hard in the factory and also do a lot of overtime to earn extra money. The cost of living there is very high, and I also have to save money to send it home. I find it difficult to adjust with the people there since their lifestyle and culture is different, but I have to adjust them because of my own needs. But fortunately there are many people from my region working here. There are many people from Pratapgarh, Jaunpur, Faizabad, Mirzapur and so on. They all work under my *seth* (labour contractor). Although I feel sad at leaving my wife and other family members behind, I have to accept the situation since it is a compulsion for me to stay in Surat and earn money. Since both my wife and I are illiterate, we cannot write letters to each other, but thankfully because of the existence of telephone facility in the village, I can ring her up once in a while and talk to her. I understand that she too is struggling hard looking after the needs of our family single-handedly. Sometimes she breaks down and cries on the telephone. But there is no way out of this situation, and we both have to face it bravely.

*Mangru, Barwaripur*[7]

My name is Mangru, and I belong to the *Chamar* caste. I am nearly seventy years old. I was born into a labourer's family. Since my family was very poor, they could not afford to send me to school, so I am totally illiterate, and I too had to work as a labourer since my childhood. When I was young the *Thakurs* owned most of the land of this village. Almost all the labourers including my father worked in their fields, and they were treated very badly by the landowners. With no other option for obtaining employment in the region, the labourers were forced to bear their exploitation in silence.

My family owns a small amount of land. After division, my share came to only two or three biswas. But this tiny amount of land is insufficient for sustaining my entire family. So once I went off to Sultanpur in search of a job without telling my wife. I found work as a labourer in a brick kiln. After that I worked for a few days in Azamgarh. I was paid Rs 20 per day in those days. In the village I was given 1.25 kilograms of grain in exchange of one day's labour, which was too little to feed my family. Even today the *Thakurs* hand over the same amount. We labourers together tried to persuade the landlords to increase the amount of grain, but they were adamant. That is why most of the men of the village including me had to migrate elsewhere for work.

When I left my family to go to Sultanpur and Azamgarh, I went with a heavy heart since my wife had to be left behind with two small children and my elderly mother to look after. So I came back home every weekend to be with her. Today my children have grown older, so there is no longer any compulsion for me to stay with her. If I get a well-paid job far away from my village, I will certainly accept it. Almost all the able-bodied men of my village have migrated. I too will not mind leaving. After all even today there is no scope for work in the village except working in the fields of the landlords. But now it is difficult to tolerate their exploitation. Even today the village has a highly feudal structure and the landowners are highly exploitative and oppressive. In spite of the increased cost of living, they still hand over the same amount that they had been doing since ages. If I go, I will certainly miss my wife, but I will not feel any suffering for her or for my other family members.

Out of fear that my sons would also be compelled to work in the fields of the landlords since they are illiterate and cannot do any other work, I had sent my elder son to Punjab and then Delhi, but he could not stay away for very long. After one year he returned to the village to be with his wife and children. When my son left the village, I was not sad to see him go, but I was worried about what he would eat and who would look after him. He had been working in brick kilns there. I used to get news about him from the other *pardesis* working with him. My wife and I used to pray to *Sati Mai* and *Jorawar Baba* to protect him and give him a long life. After he returned safely, both of us offered sweets (*kahari*) to them to thank them.

*Jorawar Baba* is the protector (*dihwar*) of our village. It is because of him that our village is safe and all the people are contented. There is also a Hanuman temple in the east of our village. It is said that when Lord Laxman was hit by a *shakti baan* (arrow), Hanuman stopped there while on his way to fetch the *Sanjeevni* plant that would cure him. A demon called Kalnem had been sent by Ravana to kill him. It was at this spot where he confronted Hanuman in order to carry out his task, dressed as a priest. When Hanuman went to the well (*kund*) nearby to take a bath, a spider living in the well informed him about his evil designs. Hanuman then killed him and was able to go and fetch the plant that brought Lord Laxman to life. Even today a fair is held every year in memory of this incident from Hindu mythology.

I have seen many things in the sixty years of my life and have also tolerated many things. Today I cannot tolerate many things, but what can I do? I had to do the work that my father did, and now my son is doing. Even today we are suffering because of being born as untouchables. Although the upper-caste people now drink water from our hands, they still make us feel like lower castes. Today I am in the last stage of my life. I just pray to *Dihwar baba* that the few years that are left to me pass off peacefully.

### *Ramashish, Majhauwa*[8]

I am not used to speaking much, so how can I narrate my life story? I will try to tell as much as I can. Ten years earlier I fell into the company of a few young boys who were on their way to Delhi to search for work. I decided to accompany them. When I asked my parents for permission, at first my mother started weeping uncontrollably. She forbade me from going, saying that we would share whatever little food was available. My father too did not like the idea of my going away. At that time, we had a small plot of land, but it was insufficient to sustain our large family. So my father used to supplement the income by doing odd jobs. But I wanted to live well rather spend my life in the village working as a daily labourer. Finally my parents gave me permission to go to Delhi.

When I first went to Delhi, I worked at making chains for tying up cows and buffaloes. I was paid Rs 25 per day for this work. The pay was so less that I could not save anything after paying for food and rent and buying necessary commodities. So I could not send any money home. I was illiterate so I could not even write letters to them.

I did this work for three years, and then I learnt the work of painting houses. I found a job as a painter, but this work too was not paying enough. So I left this job also. While I was hunting for another one, I met an old friend Ramu who suggested that I learn making objects with plaster of Paris. This would be more paying, and I would be able to save more. I learnt this work and found a job, but this too was not very paying. Now I have started working on my own. I make objects for decorating people's houses. Now I am able to send home around Rs 1,000 per month. This amount is enough to sustain my family since I don't have any children. My wife lives in the village with my parents. Sometimes when I miss my wife, my friends suggest that I should bring her with me. But setting up a household in Delhi means a lot of expenditure. The rent of the room where I am staying now is Rs 550. It is too small for my wife and me. If she comes here, I will have to hire a bigger room for which I will have to pay more.

It is very difficult to live alone in a big city like Delhi. I do my washing, cleaning and cooking myself. My workload makes it difficult for me to go to my village often to meet my family members. The first time I went back to my village after coming to Delhi was after three and a half years. The next time I went after one year. Today I go back to my village every six months. Although I live and work in Delhi, my heart is with my wife in the village. Every time I go back, she insists on accompanying me to Delhi, but each time I have to refuse. Earlier I liked my village a lot, but now I find Delhi more exciting. I can't stay in the village for very long since I miss my work and my friends. Now I am in the village to attend my sister's wedding. This is the story of my life and my struggles. Today I am contented and don't lack anything except my wife's companionship.

### Lalchand, Majhauwa[9]

My life is one long story of struggle. The struggle began when I was quite young. My father worked in the Ordinance Factory in Kanpur. I visited him once in a while, and I was very happy. But maybe God did not like me to be happy. Suddenly my father fell ill and died. All the responsibilities of the family fell on my shoulders since I was the eldest son. At that time I was in the final year of my graduation in the Maltari Degree College. This grave responsibility compelled me to give up my studies and search for a job. I went to my uncle's house in Lucknow, and asked him to find me employment. My uncle succeeded in getting me a job as a class IV staff in a factory, but I did not like the work at all. I left the job and went back to my village.

I was already married by that time, and I had to support my wife, my two younger brothers, my two unmarried sisters and my mother. Unable to find a suitable job in the village, I again went off, this time to Delhi. In Delhi I found work as an assistant to a ginger seller who had a stall in a vegetable market there. I was paid Rs 10 per day at that time. This was in 1975, and at that time this sum seemed quite a large amount. With that money I supported my entire family. I received letters regularly from my family back home, but suddenly once I did not receive any message from them for a long time. This made me very worried, and I decided to quit my job and go back to the village.

I took a train from Delhi to Allahabad, feeling desperate to go home and meet my wife and children. But it was not to be. I had filled up a form for the post of a sub-inspector of police, and the interview was scheduled to be held a few days after I reached Allahabad from Delhi. So I decided to stay there and return after the interview. I finally reached my village nearly a week after reaching Delhi. In my village I tied up with my old friend Rabindra Rai and started a shop for selling cloth. I worked at this shop for ten to twelve years.

One day a relative of ours came to my house and suggested that I join a new school that had just come up in Mustafabad, named after Dr Ambedkar. Since I had been interested in the Dalit movement, I agreed to join as a teacher. Since then I have been working in this school, and by the grace of God, I am happy here.

### Harilal, Majhauwa[10]

My name is Harilal Harijan. I am presently working in Allahabad Bank in Calcutta. Before this I was posted in Maldah, also in West Bengal. My grandmother has been living in Calcutta for a long time. My grandfather died a long time back. My family has been suffering from poverty for a long time. The condition was so bad that often we could not eat two square meals in a day. That is why in 1970 I decided to go to my grandmother's place in Calcutta and hunt for a job there. She worked as a maid in the house of a *Marwari* businessman called Gulabchand Hiralal Kanhaiyalal Dhorwil. He paid her Rs 500 each month, in return of which she dropped and fetched his children from school every day. She ran the household with this money.

I failed in high school. I studied in the village school, but when I could not pass the high school exam, I went off to my grandmother's house. At that time I was eighteen years old. My first job in Calcutta was with my uncle Rambali who worked in an iron-smelting workshop. I worked there for sometime, but my grandmother did not like my job much. My maternal uncle who worked in the labour board found me a job as a labourer in a factory. I was paid Rs 10 per day. Since I need not support any one, the amount was adequate for me.

After working there for a few days, I quit the job since it was too laborious for me. Once again I went back to my grandmother's place and asked her to find me a job. This time she took me to her *Marwari* employer and asked him to find me work. *Babuji*, as we called him, was a very kind man. He made me a part of his household retinue and gave me the job of fetching milk every day from a nearby dairy. Sometimes *Babuji* would call me home and ask me to do a few odd jobs for him. After a few months, he gave me employment in his factory where I worked for sometime.

One day *Babuji* called me to his house and asked me whether I would like to work in a bank. I replied in the affirmative. *Babuji* then fetched a form and asked me to fill it up. The GM and chairman of the bank were his good friends, and on his recommendation I got the job. After my appointment, the chairman asked me whether I would mind being posted in Maldah. I replied that I did not mind being posted anywhere. So I was sent to work in the Maldah branch of the bank.

In 1983 I was transferred back to Calcutta and I am still posted here. I work as a dispatcher. My basic salary is Rs 5,000, and altogether I get Rs 10,000. Today my economic condition is quite good, and I am satisfied with my life. The only thing that saddens me is that my family is still in the village. I cook my own food and wash my own clothes. I drink tea at the nearby tea stall. The absence of a family life really makes me feel sad. But there is no alternative since my wife has to be in the village to look after my old parents. My life in Calcutta is passing in a routine manner. When I go home to my village, I feel happy to meet my family members. With the blessings of my grandmother and *Babuji*, the acute poverty that

I experienced in my childhood is a thing of the past. Since I don't need much money in the city, I send most of my salary to my wife. Our house, which was earlier a mud cottage, has been renovated with bricks and cement. My children and other family members eat wholesome meals every day and are living comfortably. My only prayer to God is to keep everyone happy and contented and not want for anything.

The narratives of the women who have been deserted by their husbands reflect the pain and pathos of all the women of the Bhojpuri region whose husbands have migrated outside the village in search of work and money due to the lack of adequate employment facilities in the village. These women are filled with grief on being deserted from their husbands. We get to know the feelings of a deserted wife during different seasons of the year, the suffering of a deserted wife in the middle of the bed and the hardships a migrant's wife has to face in different seasons. The migrants' wives try to console themselves by saying that their husbands were compelled to go to a distant land to earn money to sustain their families lying in abject poverty and misery.

Not only do we find the pain of migration in the narratives of women but also in the narratives of men who had migrated for a living to other cities within India. The only element that forced these people to migrate was their poverty-stricken life and mounting economic pressure. It is evident from the aforementioned narratives of the deserted wives that their husbands were also not happy at their destinations. Anara, while narrating her story, said that her husband is very sad when he leaves his home. She would like to see him off at the bus station when he leaves, but he forbids her from doing so since he feels sad when he sees her sorrowful face. After leaving the house, he does not look back, otherwise he will suffer in *pardes*. No one is there to take care of their husbands in *pardes*, and the husbands suffer a great deal without their wives. The living conditions there are very bad, and after working hard the whole day the husbands have to come back home and cook their own food. Rita, in her narrative, said that in spite of having a wife her husband has to live like this, the reason being poverty and the absence of job opportunities in the village.

All these narratives of men and women also indicate that though the pain of separation is acute due to migration, the onset of technology and communication facilities has reduced this pain to some extent. Now the migrants as well as their deserted wives can be connected to each other and listen to each other's voices through mobiles and telephone facility unlike the times when the wives did not have any contact with their husbands for a long period of time and writing letters was the only mode of communication, which sometimes were also lost during transit.

## Notes

1. Interview of Geeta Nishad, Barwaripur village, by Nivedita Singh, 12 May 2005.
2. Interview of Anara, Barwaripur village, by Nivedita Singh, 13 May 2005.
3. Interview of Savitridevi, Semra village, by Nivedita Singh, 13 July 2005.
4. Interview of Rita, Majhauwa village, by Nivedita Singh, 4 August 2005.
5. Interview of Indrawati, Majhauwa village, by Nivedita Singh, 4 August 2005.
6. Interview of Chhotu, Semra village, by Nivedita Singh, 13 July 2005.
7. Interview of Mangru, Barwaripur village, by Nivedita Singh, 13 May 2005.
8. Interview of Ramashish, Majhauwa village, by Nivedita Singh, 4 August 2005.
9. Interview of Lalchand, Majhauwa village, by Nivedita Singh, 4 August 2005.
10. Interview of Harilal, Majhauwa village, by Nivedita Singh, 4 August 2005.

# 6

# MIGRATION AND CULTURAL PRODUCTIONS: DOCUMENTING HISTORY OF CULTURAL PRACTICES

*Aaile sawanwa ghar naahi re sajanwa ram*
*Hari hari dekhe bin tarse mor nayanwa re hari*
(Jagesar)
(Singh 1958: 212)

(Monsoon has arrived but my husband is not at home, O Rama.
My eyes still strain to see the greenery, O Hari.)

Migration has always been such a major human activity in the Bhojpuri region that it has become the foundational element of the culture of that society. The manifold ramifications of this phenomenon because of the emotional loss and multiple kinds of experiences of the affected persons have impacted on the memory, identity and folk psyche of the people, leading to the formation of a distinct culture. If one were to analyse the culture of the Bundelkhand and Braj regions, one would find that the basis of this culture is the migration of Lord Krishna from Mathura to Dwarka. This migration and the emotional loss caused by it has been the subject of folklore composed by saints, communities, poets and writers of this region that has mingled with the folk culture in many parts of the country. In the Awadh region as well, the exile of Lord Rama to the forest has helped in the creation of a folk culture that is the foundation of the distinctive culture of that region. The poem composed by Kalidas based on the separation of Yaksha from Yakshini has also become a symbol of the folk culture of this region (Majumder 2010: 75).

One form of cultural representation is folk songs. A popular folk song that is based on the sorrow of separation is *biraha*. *Biraha* songs are usually based on the life of people. They deal with each aspect of life like sorrow, joy, hopes and misery. They were composed by ordinary people and are the property of the folk. This folk genre is especially very popular among the Ahir caste in rural areas. The *biraha raag* (tune) that emanated from the flute of Lord Krishna when he played with the cowherdesses in Vrinadavan in the ancient period has now been transformed into the *biraha* folk song, and it is usually sung by people who look after cows and are involved in agriculture.

According to folklore expert Dr Hardev Bahri, the *biraha* songs usually consist of two lines sung in a folk tune. These songs usually described the sorrow of the *gopis* (cowherdesses) when they were separated from Lord Krishna and were popularly known as *biraha, ragini, rasiya, prasang bhagait* and so on, in the folk dialects of North India. In their present form the *biraha* folk songs are not only meant for entertainment but also commentaries on the social vices existing in society and methods of fighting with them and improving social conditions. These include issues like dowry, female feticide, untouchability, casteism, terrorism and migration.

*Biraha* folk songs are popular in regions lying in east Uttar Pradesh, west Bihar, north Madhya Pradesh, Chhattisgarh and north-eastern Jharkhand. *Biraha* has different forms like *loriki, chandaini, khari biraha* and *biraha*. Each of these forms is popular in different regions; for example the *loriki* form is popular in Awadh, Banaras, Bundelkhand, Chhattisgarh, Maithili and in the regions adjoining Nepal.

In the colonial period when the mass migration from the Bhojpuri region took place to various countries across the globe like Mauritius, Suriname, Guyana and Fiji, the migrants took with them their folk culture, as we have mentioned earlier. Folk songs like *loriki, chandaini, khari Biraha,* and *biraha* were also taken, which the migrants sang when they sat together after work. In the book *Mauritius ki Bhojpuri parampara* ('Bhojpuri tradition of Mauritius'), the author Dr Savita Buddhu writes that

> Biraha folk song has emerged from the *biraha* (separation), which describe sorrow of separation. When the people from Uttar Pradesh and Bihar arrived in their destination points, at that time Chhutta *Biraha* used to be sung. No musical instruments were used as accompaniments. There was one lead singer and the other four or five singers work as chorus singers. This tradition is found in Mauritius, Fiji, Suriname and other Caribbean countries where the migrants went.

In the present period when migration from east Uttar Pradesh, west Bihar and other Bhojpuri regions to various parts of India like Mumbai, Calcutta, Goa, Nagpur, Surat and Gurgaon is still taking place, the migrants carry with them their folk culture, of which *biraha* songs are an

*Figure 6.1* *Birha* Folk Singer Mannu Yadav Giving His Performance during a Cultural Meet. Photograph: Brijendra Gautam, January 2016

important component. In places lying in the Bhojpuri region like Lakhimpur Kheri, Lucknow, Raebareli, Kaushambi, Pratapgarh, Allahabad, Faizabad, Gonda, Basti, Deoria and Gorakhpur and in places in Madhya Pradesh like Maihar, Satna, Rewa, Sidhi, Sarguja, Bilaspur, Raipur and Durg, *biraha* is still a flourishing folk culture. Grierson, in the *Journal of Asiatic Society*, has written the following about *biraha*, 'Biraha has no particular literary value, but because the songs are symbols of the underlying feelings and aspirations of the people this form is still important. In reality Biraha is like a wild flower' (Grierson 1886: 45).

*Biraha* is the best folk composition of social harmony, which has been linked with Lord Krishna since the ancient period, and has been kept alive mainly by the Yadavs of the Hindi-speaking region of North India. Dr Krishnadev Upadhyaya in his book *Introduction to Folk Culture* has written that 'Biraha hit the heart just like the dohas of Bihari' (Yadav 2014: 10). *Biraha* is of two kinds. The first is the small *biraha*. This has only four stanzas known, which is also known as *charkariya biraha*. The other one is the big *biraha*, in which a long story from *Ramayana* or *Mahabharata* is narrated. Small *biraha* is more popular among the people. It is considered to be a part of folk culture, while the big *biraha* is considered to be a ballad. The big *biraha* includes Lorik Manjari's story, Lorik Chanda's story,

Malageet's story by Lorik and parts of *Ramayana* and *Mahabharata*, sung in the form of *biraha*.

*Biraha* can be divided into five kinds. These are:

1. Traditional *biraha: loriki, chandaili, khari biraha* (in the form of ballad)
2. Common *biraha: vandana, nirgun, ritugeet, charkariya, birhini* (in the form of folk song)
3. Literary *biraha: chhand, biraha* poem with *vidhan* (in the form of poem)
4. Elaborate *biraha:* love stories, *veer* (bravery) stories, religious stories (as small ballads)
5. Contemporary *biraha:* incidents, burning issues, issues for social change (in the form of small ballads and folk songs).

(ibid: 11)

As an oral folk culture *biraha* has been passed down over generations since the ancient period. It also includes Lorik Manjari story, Lorik Chanda story and other religious stories, which have been kept in the oral memory of the singers. In the changing context, the educated singers write down the songs, while even today the illiterate singers memorize the *biraha* songs before singing them. See figure 6.1.

It is believed that the idioms, metaphors and symbols used in the *biraha* songs in the contemporary period reflect the changing desires and aspirations of the people and are thus a repository of human emotions. In addition they are a repository of the folk wisdom of the people of different places and language groups.

According to the traditional belief regarding folk songs, the singers use the *ragas kaharwa, khemta, dadra, deepchandi* and so on, depending on their particular style. They are usually accompanied by musical instruments like *kartal, manjira* and *jhanjh*. See figure 6.2. Dholak and harmonium are used alongside. In the Allahabadi style the *biraha* singers also use *nagara* while singing. In the eastern *chhapariya*, the singers use *chaita, kajri, nayakwa, belwariya, chaulriya, chautal* and *alha* tunes for singing *biraha* songs. Some popular forms of *biraha* songs are *kajari, alha, kaubali, sohar, poorvi, chhaparhiya, dhobiyukt geet, gorau geet, kaharwa, paita, chaulriya, belwariya, nayakwa, khemta, birhini, nirgun, gari* (wedding songs), *pachra, bidesia, jhoomar, lachari, piriya geet, sorthhi brijbhar, thhunmuniya kajari, dadra, ghato* and *jantsar*. All the nine *rasas* like *shringar ras, hasya ras, karun ras, veer ras, raudras, bhayanak ras, vibhats ras, adbhutras* and *shant ras* are used in *biraha* songs. Some famous *biraha* singers who have helped to spread this form among the people are Sri Chhedi Yadav, Ram Khelawan Yadav, Pujari Hiralal Yadav, Ram Kailash Yadav, Babu Ram Yadav, Jhillu Kushwaha, Ram Awadh Yadav, Ballu Yadav, Ram Dev Yadav, Parashuram Yadav, Shivmurat

*Figure 6.2* Folk Singer Mannu Yadav Performing *Birha* Using *Kartal*. Photograph: Brijendra Gautam, January 2016

Yadav, Kashinath Yadav, Ram Naresh Yadav and Vishwanath Yadav. Many of them are invited to give performances in places where large populations of Bhojpuri migrants have settled.

Another popular Bhojpuri folk song genre is *poorbi*. The meaning of the word *poorbi* is 'from the poorab or east'. Its actual meaning in Hindi is 'originating from the east'. While defining *poorbi*, Dr Sanjay Kumar Singh says that 'The songs that were sung in the eastern districts of the Bhojpuri region were called poorbi.' Among all the Bhojpuri folk genres, *poorbi* is one of the most popular and the *poorbi* songs are characterized by a high-pitched wail that imparts the element of sorrow in them. These songs are sung from the Poorvanchal region of Uttar Pradesh to the western part of Bihar. Their roots are considered to be in the Shahabad and Saran regions of Bihar, but they are popular over a large area in Uttar Pradesh and Bihar. Apart from Uttar Pradesh and Bihar, *poorbi* songs are sung in Bengal, Orissa, Assam and several other places including overseas. However, they have definitely originated in the Bhojpuri region since the Bhojpuri culture is strongly reflected in these songs. They are also continually evolving according to the region and singer.

There is another opinion regarding *poorbi* songs among Bhojpuri folklore experts that says that *poorbi* songs and tunes are linked with a particular job and profession. They believe that *poorbi* is the song of only those people who go to the east (*poorab*) for job or business. The separation of these people from their native lands gave birth to this genre. The reason for this is that most *poorbi* songs have a mention of the east in them. For example,

> *hari mora gaile ho poorbi banijiya ho ram*
> *e rama duara pe lage navrangaya ho* ram[1]

> Translation
>
> My husband has gone to the Poorab region, O Rama
> I have decorated Rangoli at the door of my house, O Rama

In general, however, ordinary people consider *poorbi* and *bidesia* to be the same but there is a minute difference between the two. *Poorbi* songs have a high-pitched wail in them, while *bidesia* songs have no wailing aspect. A popular *poorbi* song sung by famous Bhojpuri singer Sharda Sinha is:

> *Paniya ki jahaj palarniya ho mein jaiha piya*
> *Aare le le aiha ho piya jhulni bangal ke*[2]

> Translation
>
> My husband set sail to a distant land in a ship
> O my husband bring for me the Jhumkas of Bengal

*Poorbi* singers have also tried out several improvisations with the songs at different places. Many local singers have added the *poorbi* tune in the singing of *Ramayana* in the Shahabad district of the Bhojpuri region of Bihar. In addition to the element of sorrow of separation that underlie these songs, they have added social, political, economic and other themes in them to make them more relevant to the listeners.

*Poorbi* songs are also found in the districts of Gorakhpur, Basti and Jaunpur in Uttar Pradesh, but the characteristic tune of *poorbi* that is present in the Bihari Bhojpuri districts is not found there. There is a great difference between the element of sorrow found in *poorbi* songs and that found in other Bhojpuri folk song genres. The sorrow at the separation of two lovers is the most important element in them. One *poorbi* song describes the sorrow of a wife whose husband brings her home after marriage but migrates soon after:

*gavana karval e hari ji*
*apne bideswa gaile ho ram*[3]

*Translation*

My husband after my gauna brought me to his home
And he himself went to a foreign land

In the *poorbi* form, not much importance is given to the classical beat and *raag*. Bhojpuri folk singers do not have much knowledge about the grammar of music, and they consider tune to be the *raag*. While classical music is heavily based on beat and *raag*, folk songs are based more on tune and emotions. *Poorbi* folk songs are also not bound by the element of time and can be sung at all times, on all festivals and in all regions. It is a form that narrates the emotions between husbands and wives like their attraction, their small quarrels and their sorrow at separation, and their social and economic ramifications.

Bholanath Gahamari in his book *Lok Ragini (Bhojpuri Kavya)* says that *poorbi* has several forms that are not known to many people. A few of them like *aam poorbi, chhaprahiya* and *patnahiya* are common, but others like *darun poorbi, chappai poorbi* and *dhannarh poorbi* are not very common. In the folk language it is said that

*ahakan, dahaka, darun, lahakan*
*chatkan, sant hanker*
*chahakan, binhan, mannat lalkari*
*poorbi nau prakar*[4]

This says that *poorbi* has nine forms, for example *ahakan*, which is based on ego; *dahakan*, in which there is separation; *darun*, in which there are social, political and economic sorrows; *lahakan*, in which there are jealousy, anger and so on; *chatakan*, in which there is satire on reforms; *sant hanker*, which describes formless god; *chahakan*, in which there is humour; *binhak*, which touches the heart; and *mannat lalkari*, in which there is joy, enthusiasm and bravery.[5]

Another popular Bhojpuri folk song genre is *kajari*, which comprises songs based on the monsoon season. This form holds a special place in Bhojpuri folklore and has been defined and explained by several experts on Bhojpuri folklore. The basic meaning of *kajari* is 'the song in which there is water fall when it is sung', that is they are songs that are sung in the monsoon season.

*Kajari* songs contain words and *raags* that describe sorrow due to separation, attraction for women and their jewellery and so on. For example,

> man bhave gahana garhai d balmu
> piya patne ka paijeb chandi auwal hum leb
> nepal se hamai nathiya mangai d balamu
> ho mangai da balamu
> manbhave gahana. . . .

*Translation*

> Please get my desired ornaments o my husband
> O My husband I will take the silver anklets made in Patna
> Bring my nose ring from Nepal, o my husband
> Get my desired ornaments, O my husband

*Kajari* songs are believed to have been originally formed in Mirzapur. These songs were specially sung in wrestling rings (*akhara*). Since the last few years, women have also been entering the wrestling ring *kajari* song sessions, which can be seen as a sign of their empowerment and identity formation. The women discourse has usually been presented by the *kajari akharas*, of which the most famous is the *Latarani ka akhara*. This *akhara* is very popular among women in Mirzapur.

If we pay attention to the metres of *kajari*, we will find that the main metres are *kakahara, nakhshikh, ekangmisra, bandsarpa, halakband* and *adharchhand*. In the *bandsarpa* form there is a description of the parts of the body from head to toe. In the *halakband* form the songs are sung without moving the tongue. In the *adharchhand* form the lips are not moved since the sounds produced by the lips are not used in them.

*Kajari* songs are developing and evolving continually. At present there are several poets who are composing *kajari* songs in different forms. In the *kajari* performances one can see both the beauty of emotions, language and style of the songs and the beauty of the voices and tunes of the singers.

Another Bhojpuri folk song genre is the *barahmasa*. There are two traditions for writing Hindi love poems. The first is the description of the six seasons, and the other is of the twelve months. While the poems based on the six seasons have been produced by the classical poetry tradition, the poems and songs based on the twelve months (*barahmasa*) are a production of the folk. However, the barahmasa folklore form has now been incorporated and included in the Hindi love-based poems genre.

Being a folklore form, the barahmasa genre is an oral tradition that is a repository of love-based compositions. The songs and poems included in the barahmasa are usually based on the theme of separation, which is sung by the lovelorn wife who is left behind at home by her migrant husband. The songs are based on the twelve Indian months, namely *Asharh, Sawan, Bhadon, Kunwar, Kartik, Agahan, Poos, Maah (Maagh), Phagun, Chait, Baisakh* and *Jeth*. Some *barahmasa* also include descriptions of the *Laud* month, and these songs are called *terahmasi* by poets.

The *barahmasa* songs usually describe the pain and pathos undergone by a woman whose husband is away and who cannot celebrate the various festivals and participate in the rituals associated with them that are performed with great joy by the other women. The songs give a vivid description of the beauty of the season when the festival is celebrated, the sounds of the birds and the beauty of nature. A song that describes the mental condition of a single woman during the month of *Asharh* is given here:

> *Aya maas asharh ka peetam nahi paas*
> *Ghatar ghatae det hai pi darshan ki aas*
> *Asharh aya ghata chhai gagan par*
> *Risawat man mora rasiya sajan ghar*
> *Sakal chaumas chhav apne ghar ko*
> *Piya mein chhaya jane kis nagar ko*
> *Bharan parhti hai tum phenk jae mera*
> *Piya bin jag hua moko andhera*
> *Parhe ho boond mere tan tape par*
> *Taran mit jaye jyon tapte tabe par*
> (Kadri)

*Translation*

> The month of Aashad has arrived and my dear husband is not with me
> I am longing for my husband but the hope of meeting him is gradually diminishing
> The sky is filled with clouds in Aashad
> My heart is paining because my husband is not at home
> Everyone is covering their house in these four months
> But I don't know my husband is there in which land
> The fields are uncultivated yet and my heart is also in the same situation

The world seems dark to me without my husband
Raindrops are falling on my burning body
To soothe the pain of my body

In another song based on the month of *Saawan*, a sorrow-filled woman describes her condition to her friends in the following manner:

*Sakhi hans-hans sunawen tujhe pi saath*
*Main ro-ro man ke tej mein malun haath*
*Main gam ke palne mein khaun jhauke*
*Sunayun kisko main birha gheeke*

Translation

My friends laugh and say that I should be near my husband
And I cry and rub my hands in the fire that burns my heart
My heart is full of misery and pain
To whom should I narrate my pain of separation

The feelings of the woman are expressed in the following way:

*Sakhi pi bin nahi hai chain moko*
*Kathin hai katna din rain moko*

Translation

O my friend I am restless without my husband
Days and nights have become difficult to pass

A *barahmasa* describing the month of *Kunwar* is as follows:

*Sagara kunwar gujar gaya piyon na phera keen*
*Karwari si bhaithi rahi bhag hamare peen*
*Bhara chaumas bhar birha ka dukhrha*
*Abhi tak tune dikhlaya na mukhrha*

Translation

The month of Kunwar has gone and my husband has not yet returned
I kept sitting with my arms open wide for my husband but my destiny is painful

For whole twelve months I have borne the pain of separation
But O my husband you have not shown me your face as yet

A *barahmasa* describing a woman's feelings before the coming of Diwali is as follows:

*Diwali ke diye bare hai nari*
*Main hoon mandir ke ujiyare se nari*
*Sabhi bare hain ghar-bahar diyari*
*Diya mera barh kin kar diyari*
*Sabhi bakhri pate hain mit nagari*
*Meri bhakhri mein sagari dhool bikhari*
                                    (ibid)

*Translation*

The earthen lamps have been decorated in Diwali
I am a woman who glows through the light of the temple
Everyone is decorating their houses with earthen lamps
Who will light the lamps of my heart
All the houses of the city are filled with joy
But in my house there is dust and dirt all over

A song describing a woman's feelings on seeing her friends enjoying Holi in the season of spring with their husbands is as follows:

*Ye tesu phoolon phagun ke watan mein*
*Mere likhe lagti aag tan mein*
*Malain hai sab gulal apas mein much se*
*Hanse bole piya ke sang such se*
*Main dekhoon hoon kinhi ko khelte phaag*
*Mere tan mein lagi hai dekhkar aag*
                                    (ibid)

*Translation*

The month of Phagun has come and the Tesu flowers have started growing
As I am writing my heart and mind is burning with pain
Everyone is applying gulal on their bodies
They are laughing and enjoying with their husbands
When I see others playing Holi
My heart is filled with sorrow and I feel jealous

*Barahmasa* songs do not mention the person who is being addressed but rather address the birds that are requested to act as messengers. A *barahmasa* addressed to crows is as follows:

> *Main sunder shyama ban kab tak rahoon ri*
> *Daurkar jo kaga se kahoon ri*
> *Ki jhatpat kaarh kar mero kaleja*
> *Ye hai pati piya ke paas le ja*
>
> (ibid)

*Translation*

> Till when I should maintain myself and look beautiful
> I should run and say to the crow
> Take my heart to my husband
> Take this letter to my husband

Another *barahmasa* song based on the month of *Asharh* is as follows:

> *Asharh aya ghata chhai gagan par*
> *Rasawat man mora rasiya sajan par*
> *Sakal chahumas chhawat apne ghar ko*
> *Piya ne chhay jane kis nagar ko*
> *Jahan mein chhan sab charwa rahe hain*
> *Hamari chhan badal chha rahe hain*
> *Hui taiyar sabag ki chhan ghar ki*
> *Mere ghar chhai bauchhahon ki sirki*
>
> (ibid)

Another Bhojpuri folk song genre is *jantsar*. *Jantsar* songs are also known as *shram* (labour) songs as they are sung by workers in chorus when they are working. These songs are usually based on agriculture and other labour activities like grinding wheat or paddy in the grinding wheel (*jantsar*), sowing and harvesting. The Bhojpuri region is a labour-oriented society where people are mostly engaged in agriculture and other labour activities and the workers like to sing while working. This has given rise to a distinct folk song genre that describes these various activities. Interestingly most of the songs describe the labour activities of women, and these songs are usually sung by women while working.

*Jantsar* songs are mainly sung while rotating the stick in a grinding wheel when grinding wheat. The word *jantsar* has two parts, *jant* and *sar*. *Jant* is the name for the grinding wheel on which wheat is ground to produce wheat flour (*atta*). *Sar* means home or place. Thus *jantsar* songs are songs that are sung in the room where wheat is ground. These songs describe the hard and painful labour undergone by women who grind wheat in the heavy grinding wheel. These songs have no embellishments or decorations but describe the harsh realities of life. There is a beautiful rhythm between these songs and the work being done. The ragas on which these songs are based are stretched only till one move of the wheel. Like folklore, these songs also differ from time, place and singer, and the *raags* also change according to the dialect used in a particular place.

*Jantsar* songs are categorized according to the quality and quantity of the wheat.

> *Akhar ganhuake chhti-chhoti jhikiya*
> *Seedhwa girela jhajhkari nure rama*
> *Hathwa pirai jab janghiya pirile*
> *Munhwa se chute jantsar nure ram*
> *Saasu gaawe serahi nanad mor paserhi*
> *Ta gotini duserhi ke raag nu re ram*
> (Tiwari 2013: 49)

*Translation*

I am grinding wheat in the grinding wheel
The flour is falling below gradually
My hands and thighs are paining
And in this situation I am expressing my pain by singing *jantsar*
My mother in law sings *serahi* while my sister in law sings *paserhi*
And my Jethani (my husband's brother's wife) is singing in a different tune.

We can divide *jantsar* into the following kinds: *chhatkahi, pavahi, serhi, duserhi, teen serhi* and *paserhi*. Like other folk songs Bhojpuri *jantsar* also reflects the contemporary social and political scenario of the Bhojpuri region and also of the time when they were originally written. There is also a reflection of the economic conditions. When they were originally written, there were three ways of earning money: through agriculture, through service and through business. In *jantsar* songs there is a lot of description about service since the heroes of many of these songs used to migrate to other cities in search of jobs.

> *Beniya besahait taka chari lagle*
> *Are gotwa jokhit bechaile re ji*
> (ibid: 75)

In *jantsar* songs there are also mentions of education since there are descriptions of writing letters and reading them. At that time letters were written on cloth, and kohl (*kajal*) worked as ink. The letters used to be delivered by migrants who used to travel to and fro (*batohi*), as well as the businessmen who went to the cities for their business work.

*Balam bidesia*

*Gahuan ke rotiya bidesia chalhawa re macchariya*
*Jeun na lehun bidesia, hamron re bhojaniya*
*Hum tohi se poochhhi bidesia, dilwa ke ram batiya*
*Kaise-kaise rahal bidesia hakim ke re naukariya*
(ibid: 98)

*Jantsar* songs are a beautiful blend of labour, artistry and music. These songs are mainly based on decoration and compassion. Love, separation, mental and physical pain and family conflicts are the major issues of these songs. The songs were usually meant for reducing physical pain and mental sufferings. They usually emerged from the feelings of women who ground wheat on the *jaant* (grinding wheel).

1  *Gawana karai bidesia ghare baithwale*
   *Kekra par chhorle bidesia anna-dhan re sonwa*
   *Kekra par chhorle bidesia vari re umariya*
   *Amma par chhorli ye dhanian anna-dhan re sonwan*
   *Chhotka bhaiawa par chhorli ye dhaniyan vari re umiriya*
(Singh 1991: 17)

2  *Peepara ke pat par phulugina dole re nanadi*
   *Purub ke des begliniya hauni ye nanadi*
   *Ahi oskhan tohar bhaiya bhetli ye nanadi*
   *Are bheji deti ghajipur chalaniya ye nanadi*
   *Hathe ke anguliya banhakiya dharbon ye bhabhi*
   *Are aapan bhaiya lebon chhorai mori bhabhi*
(ibid: 21)

3  *Naika je chalela bideswan ye sakhiya ho*
   *Dei gaile chanana machiswa ye sakhia ho*
   *Dei gaile navrang kakahiya ye sakhiya ho*
   *Ketna mai baitho ketna jhnakho bidesia re*
(ibid: 26)

The amount of sorrow that is found in *jantsar* songs is possibly not found in any other folksong genre. Labour songs are of two kinds: those sung by women and those sung by men. Whereas labour songs sung by men contain more aggression and also humour, labour songs sung by women contain naturalness, complaints against mother-in-law and sister-in-law, complaints about co-wives and pain and sorrow at the migration of husbands. The rhythm of the labour songs of men is faster, matching the rhythm of their work, while the rhythm of the labour songs of women is slower, matching their emotions and sorrow.

Apart from the folk songs related to migration, another form of cultural representation can be seen in the oral, visual and ritual domains, which is why migration should not be seen only as an economic activity but also as a cultural phenomenon. These cultural representations help the migrants and their loved ones who have been left behind to overcome the emotional loss caused by the migration. These cultural representations include various kinds of rituals, superstitions, customs and practices. Praying to God for the long life and well-being of the loved ones is one of the ways for the people who have been left behind to find solace. When colonial migration was at its peak, a goddess called *Sankata Mata* emerged in the Banaras region whom people, especially women, worshipped for the safety of their husbands or sons. She is supposed to be one of the incarnations of Goddess Durga, the most important Hindu goddess. This goddess is also known to grant all the wishes and remove all the sorrows and obstacles (*sankat*) in the lives of her devotees, especially women, who faithfully pray to her. A large temple has been built in her honour in Banaras. See figure 6.3. During the colonial period, the wives, mothers and other family members of the migrants used to come and pray before her idol for the safe return of their loved ones. Today, although the family members of migrants going to destinations within India still pray at her temple, the largest numbers of devotees are those who are facing some obstacles in their lives and come to pray for their quick removal. A tract called *Sampoorna manokamnaon ko dene wali evam sheeghra sankat nivarani Sankata Mata Vrat Katha* (fast and prayer for *Sankata Mata*, the goddess who grants all desires and quickly removes all obstacles)[6] is sold in front of the temple. The tract includes a special paean in her honour called *Mata Sankata Vrat Katha*, which all the devotees must read. The tract also details the procedure for praying to her, that is which day to pray to her, how to conduct the fast in her honour, what are the offerings that must be made to her and how many women should be invited to the prayer meeting. The tract also includes bhajans or devotional songs composed in her honour (Majumder 2010: 77).

*Figure 6.3 Sankata Mata* Temple in Varanasi Where Women Go to Offer Prayers for the Well-Being of Their Migrant Husbands

The paean in the honour of *Sankata Mata*, which every devotee must read on Friday every week as a part of the procedure of praying to her, is in the form of a story, which is as follows:

In village Jagatpur there lived an old woman. She had a young son called Ramanath. He went to Pardes to earn a living. After her son left the old woman was very sad. This was because her daughter-in-law took advantage of Ramnath's absence to continuously abuse and insult her. Everyday the old woman used go and sit in front of a well outside the village and cry. One day a goddess in the human form of 'Deepu ki Maan' (Deepu's mother) emerged from the well, which was the abode of gods and goddesses. She asked the old woman, 'O old woman, why do you sit in front of this well everyday and cry? What is your sorrow? Please tell me your sadness. I will try to remove it. (ibid: 79)

The old woman, however, did not reply and kept sitting silently. But when Deepu's mother kept persisting she said, 'Why do you keep asking me? Can you really remove my sorrow when you learn of it?'

On this Deepu's mother replied, 'I will try my best to do so.' When the old woman received this assurance she let out her pent up sorrow to her. She said, 'My son has gone to Pardes to earn money. In his absence my daughter-in-law always abuses me. This is the reason for my sorrow.'

After hearing the old woman, Deepu's mother said, 'Not far from this village, inside the forest, there is a temple of Sankata Mata. You can tell her your story and beg her to relieve you of your sorrow. She is very kindhearted. She can make poor people rich, bless childless couples with children, strengthen weak people and make luckless people lucky. With her blessings married woman always remain in the married state. Virgin girls get good husbands and sick people become healthy. Apart from these, she grants the innermost desires of all her devotees.' (ibid)

The old woman immediately went to the temple of Sankata Mata, fell at the feet of the idol and started weeping. Sankata Mata's heart filled with kindness. She asked the old woman, 'O old woman, what is the sorrow for which you are always weeping?'

The old woman replied, 'Mata, my son has gone to Pardes. In his absence his wife is always abusing me. Her behaviour has become intolerable. That is why I keep crying.'

Sankata Mata then assured her saying, 'Don't worry. You go back home and feed seven married women. Your son will soon return safe and sound.'

The old woman went back and did as she was told. After a few days her son returned and her life once again filled with joy. (ibid: 79)

Reading this paean is an integral part of the ritual of worshipping *Sankata Mata*. All women whose husbands and sons have gone to *pardes* go to the temple; read this paean; offer coconut, a red veil, sweets, flowers and donations of money before the idol and pray for the long life and well-being of their loved ones. With the help of donations made by the devotees, her temple has become a massive ornate one with marble floors and marble tiles. For twenty four hours the priests chant prayers and hymns in her honour and the temple is always thronging with devotees who offer prayers to her and pray for her blessings (ibid).

## *Daak Main*

The phenomenon of migration has given birth to many kinds of gods and goddesses as an outcome of the emotional need of the people left behind to ensure the well-being of their loved ones and because of the insecurity that surrounds their absence. Each region that has witnessed mass migration causing a void in society has also invented a symbol to which they turn for succour. In village Semra, the people have invented a goddess called *Dihwarin Main* (village goddess placed at the entrance of the village believed to protect the village). She is supposed to be having six sisters, one of whom is called *Daak Main* (goddess of message). Some of the others are *Panmati, Bhanmati* and *Kalimai*. The people, especially women of that village, pray to *Daak Main* so that she sends messages from their husbands. The vehicle of *Daak Main* is the postal van that brings letters to the local post office (ibid: 81).

The ritual that is followed for praying to *Daak Main* is that women prepare meals comprising *puris, rasiaw* and *batasa*. When the postal van comes to the village, they throw the food on the van. The common belief is that unless they do so, the village will be struck with cholera and the cattle too will be affected. The villagers say that it happened once. Thus secular belief is changed in to religious belief through fear. Every year a fair of *Dihawarin Main* during *Navratri* is organized in the village in which the visitors serve food to all seven sisters. The food laid out for *Daak Main* is thrown over the postal van. Earlier this ritual was performed only by the family members of migrants but has now spread among all ladies who hope to get their wishes fulfilled (ibid).[7]

In Barwaripur village, from where many men migrate to places like Delhi, Calcutta and Mumbai, a goddess called *Murkathhi Devi* is very popular. Women pray to her to ensure that their husbands do not fall ill at their destination points. *Murkathhi Devi* is supposed to be a sati, that is a woman who sacrifices her life for her husband by burning herself at his funeral pyre. The ritual for praying to her is that a clay wok, made by the potters of the village, is placed in front of her. The wok has a pair of lizards and a lamp carved on its backside, and it is placed inverted. These symbols are good omens meant to keep bad things away from the person in whose name the wok has been moulded. Flowers, sweets, a little amount of rice, incense sticks, and so on are also placed before the idol. The women pray to the goddess with folded hands for the long life and well-being of their husbands. As in the case of *Sankata Mata* and *Daak Main*, the belief in this goddess has now spread among other women also, who pray to her for the fulfilment of their secular desires (ibid).[8]

## Beliefs

The need to fill up the emotional void created by the migration of the menfolk and ensure their long life and well-being has led the women of Barwaripur to believe a number of superstitions about their husbands. They believe that when a bird called *shuklain* (local name of a bird) calls, the husband will come home to them bearing money and gifts. When a green spider climbs up one's left shoulder, then the husband will bring items for makeup (*shauk-shringaar ke samaan*). A black spider, on the other hand, does not specify anything special. If a woman's left palm itches, it is a good omen while the itching of the right palm is a bad omen. If a woman dreams of small fishes or of a snake striking someone, it is a good sign. All the women of this village whose husbands are away take these dreams and superstitions very seriously since they are all worried about the well-being of their husbands and would like them to return soon bearing gifts for them (ibid: 84). These superstitions and beliefs have been coming down over generations and were present in the Bhojpuri region during the colonial period when overseas migration was at its peak.

## Notes

1 Interview of Dr Ramnarayan Tiwari, Gazipur, Uttar Pradesh at Patna by Badri Narayan dated 13 December 2014.
2 Ibid.
3 Ibid.
4 Ibid.

5 Ibid.
6 Edited by Swarna Padak Sammanit, Chalisa Samrat, Kavi Shiromani, Kavyan Kalanidhi Shri Ram Sundar Das 'Brahma', published by Shri Durga Pustak Bhandar, Pvt. Ltd 527 A/2, Kakkad Nagar (Dariyabad), Allahabad Branch – Johnstonganj, Allahabad.
7 Interview of villagers of Semra by Nivedita Singh, 13 July 2005.
8 Interview of villagers of Barwaripur by Nivedita Singh, 13 May 2005.

# 7

# MIGRATION AND POLITICS

*Purab Mat Jao More Saiyyan*
*Wohin Re Purubva Ki Baanki Bangalniya*
*Jadua Daari Rakhiyen More Rama Re*
                    (Shayar Shahwan)
                    (Singh 1958: 209)

Do not go to a distant land, my lord.
There lives a beautiful Bengali lass.
She will mesmerize you locked in her beauty, O my lord.

In order to understand how and why elections are drawing migrants back to their homelands to cast votes and how the phenomenon of migration impacts these places, we visited two villages in Jaunpur district, which lies in the Poorvanchal region of Uttar Pradesh. The first was Hasrauli village in Jaunpur district, which is located at a distance of 1 km from Lalabazaar on the Jaunpur–Machhlishahar road, and the second was the Baderi (Barkapur village), which is situated close to Machhlishahar, a development block in Jaunpur district. See figure 7.1.

Jaunpur is the gateway to the Bhojpuri region as it lies on the borders of Uttar Pradesh and Bihar. It is a large district having twenty-one blocks, six *tehsils* and twenty-seven thanas. Located in the northwest of Varanasi and Allahabad, its frontiers begin around forty-five kilometres from Allahabad and thirty kilometres from Varanasi. Along with Allahabad, Varanasi and Mirzapur, Jaunpur is an important location in the Poorvanchal region of Uttar Pradesh. Jaunpur is gradually emerging as an important cultural centre for Bhojpuri music and entertainment as several popular Bhojpuri singers and composers belong to this district, and it was the location for many Bhojpuri films and serials. Jaunpur city and district are also important politically as there is a high level of political awareness among the people and the region has impacted both Uttar Pradesh and national politics.

Hasrauli village is mainly dominated by people belonging to the Yadav community who number 3,000 in total. The other communities living here are Chamar (1,000); Brahmin (200); Thakur (700); and Bind, Kahar, Dhobi and so on (300). Most of the villagers are dependent on agriculture for a living, but because of the shortage of irrigation facilities, the income of most families is supplemented by the earnings sent back by their family members who have migrated to other cities for work. Nearly 80 per cent of the youth of this village have migrated to cities like Mumbai, Delhi and Surat.

The migration of people from this region to other cities within India has led to a great deal of political awareness among the people of this region, which is evident both in the homeland and in the destination points. The issue of migration was also found to figure strongly in the elections and in the political scenario, and almost all the political parties were loudly playing *bidesia* and migration songs at the important tea stalls

*Figure 7.1* Village Women Happily Narrating Their Folk Cultural Forms, in Baderi Village, Jaunpur District, Uttar Pradesh, India. Photograph: Brijendra Gautam, November 2015

and crossings. These songs touch all the villagers emotionally as migration is a harsh reality for almost every person of this village.

In our conversations with the villagers of Hasrauli, we found that there were mixed reactions about the contestants and political parties fighting these elections. Their exposure to the functioning of political parties outside their villages through their relatives who had migrated to places like Mumbai had led them to form their own opinion regarding the various political parties. Many people having relatives living and working in Mumbai were found to support the Congress party and were critical of the people who were supporting Bharatiya Janata Party (BJP) since their ally, the Shiv Sena in Maharashtra, had beaten up and driven away their relatives in Mumbai a few years ago. On the other hand, the BJP supporters told us that although their relatives in Mumbai are insulted and humiliated by the local people there who refer to them by the derogatory terms *bhaiya* and *mama*, they do not want to cause any further problems to them and so they would like to vote for BJP.

In Baderi or Barkapura, which was the other village in Jaunpur district where we visited, which is approximately one kilometre from the main road connecting Jaunpur and Machhlishahar, we found that here too migration was a burning issue. Almost every household had at least one or two members who had migrated to other cities, especially Mumbai, to work. In Mumbai most of the migrants worked as auto or taxi drivers, while the people who were left behind depended on agriculture for their livelihood. None of the people were engaged in government jobs.

In this village too we found a spirit of festivity because of the forthcoming elections, with loudspeakers loudly blaring migration songs. BJP appeared to be the popular choice for the people. In the village we also met the families of some Muslim youth who had migrated to Surat for work and had narrated glowing tales of the progress of the city. These people too supported BJP in anticipation of a rise in the overall development level, despite the negative reaction that most Muslims felt towards Narendra Modi.

The migrants usually visit their villages on important festivals like Holi and Diwali. From the living standards of the villagers, it appeared that the migrants remitted an adequate amount of money from their workplaces since almost all households possessed several consumer goods like TV, fridge and mobiles. However, the educational level of the village is not very high, especially for girls, which might be because of both the absence of institutes of higher education in the vicinity and the conservative mindset of the people, which prevents girls from travelling long distances to study. The young girls were found to be quite technologically savvy, and each girl possessed sophisticated mobiles with Internet connectivity with which she downloaded and listened to the latest film songs.

Migration is an important issue among the contestants who fight the elections from different political parties. It was observed during the 2014 Parliamentary elections that among the five contestants who stood during the elections from the Jaunpur district, several had a history of migration. The Congress Party had fielded Ravi Kishan, the BSP had fielded Subhash Pandey, the Samajwadi Party had fielded Paras Nath Yadav, the Aam Aadmi Party had fielded K.P. Yadav and the BJP had fielded K.P. Singh.

Among all the candidates who are contesting the elections, the most well-known one is Ravi Kishan (born Ravi Kishan Shukla), who is representing the Congress Party. He is a popular Bhojpuri and Hindi film and TV star who was born in a village in Jaunpur district but later migrated to Mumbai where he has now become a celebrity. Known as the Amitabh Bachchan of Bhojpuri cinema, he has acted in several Bhojpuri and Hindi films and TV shows. Talking about his interest in politics, Ravi Kishan says that although he is now settled in Mumbai he is concerned about the lack of infrastructure and development in Jaunpur, which is one of the most backward regions of Uttar Pradesh. He wants to develop Jaunpur as a shooting hub for Bhojpuri cinema by building basic infrastructure there. His priorities also include constructing toilets in each household, a stadium and a theatre centre.

Of the other contestants, Subhash Pandey from the BSP is also a former migrant who amassed a lot of money at his workplace and has now returned to Jaunpur. He was the MLA from Machhlishahar from BSP, but now he is fighting for becoming an MP. Having a history of migration, the local people also identify with him. With migration being a major issue in Jaunpur, there will be a tough competition among all the contestants in these elections since almost all the contestants have histories of migration and can understand the emotions of the villagers.

### Migrant folklore and politics in destination point

In order to study how migration from the Bhojpuri region is impacting politics at the destination points, we visited Mumbai recently to observe the scenario in localities dominated by Bhojpuri migrants like Nala Sopara, Basai, Virar, Kandivali, Borivali, Andheri and Dadar. All these regions are heavily populated by Bhojpuri migrants who work in various kinds of menial jobs. Because of their large number, the migrants emerged as an important category for all the political parties who understood their power to sway in the 2014 parliamentary elections. Since the migrants live in extreme poverty and misery as most of their earnings are remitted to their homelands, all these regions are mired in squalor and pollution and there is a complete absence of infrastructural facilities. Encashing this issue, all the political parties promise to provide them good living conditions including drinking water, electricity, roads and other facilities in order to mobilize them to vote for their party.

Just before elections almost all the political parties in the fray organize political rallies where all the Bhojpuri migrants gather in large numbers. All the political parties have realized the power of Bhojpuri folk culture to draw migrants to political meetings, and thus each party has roped in popular Bhojpuri singers to sing songs that are interspersed with requests to vote for the particular party.

We attended one such political rally organized by the Congress Party on 19 April 2014 in the Kranti Nagar rickshaw stand in the Lokhandvala township of Kandivali east, Mumbai. The chief minister of Maharashtra, Sri Prithviraj Chauhan, and the then sitting Congress MP Sanjay Nirupam from that region, who was once again standing for election, were scheduled to address the rally. Sanjay Nirupam is originally from Bihar, and all the migrants from the Bhojpuri region identify strongly with him. In order to attract a large crowd, it had been announced that a few famous

*Figure 7.2* Bhojpuri Singer Dinesh Lal Yadav 'Nirhauwa' Giving His Performance at the Time of Elections in Mumbai. Photograph: Brijendra Gautam, October 2014

Bhojpuri singers like Priyanka Singh, Nirhua and Anil Yadav would also be present to sing Bhojpuri songs. See figure 7.2.

We found that nearly 20,000 people were gathered at the venue, and just before the arrival of the two leaders the singers took the stage and start belting out popular Bhojpuri folk songs, which pulled even more people from the adjoining regions. All the songs were based on migration and described the separation from the homelands and the sorrow of the wives left behind, relying heavily on the memories of the migrants. The lyrics of one such song was *jainhe naukri pe agiye se na kahiye balamji / thori chhutti leke aur kuchh din rahiye balamji . . . kaise din rat-rat katihe hamar, kahiye balamji / ghar chhutti leke aur kuchh din rahiye balamji* (don't say in future that you will go for your job / take some more days' leave, my beloved / how I pass my nights, tell me my beloved / take some more days' leave and stay at home for a few more days my beloved).

As the intensity of the songs increased, the crowd started swaying with the music and a wave of energy ran through it. Taking advantage of the mood of the audience, the singers started praising the Congress Party in Bhojpuri language and appealed to the people to vote for Sanjay Nirupam, which would enable him to win with a large majority.

Thus at both the homeland and the destination points, we found that Bhojpuri folk culture, which is heavily dependent on the issue of migration, is one of the most significant, if not the most significant, forms to politically mobilize people of the Bhojpuri region. With migrants emerging as an important category at the destination points, which can impact political equations, arousing memories of their homelands through folk songs is an effective way of appropriating them, while in the homelands too, folk songs based on migration are used to evoke the sentiments of the people for whom migration is a lived reality. It remains to be seen if the emotional issue of migration is enough to mobilize migrants and their families or whether economic issues are also important for them.

# CONCLUSION

In the nineteenth and early twentieth centuries, after the abolishment of slavery from the world, a massive emigration took place from the Bhojpuri region to European colonies that were in need of manpower on their plantations. In India, economic depression was taking place all over the country due to the decline of weaving industries caused by the Industrial Revolution in England and by the extreme population pressure on agriculture and cultivable lands. This pressure on the resources of the country, combined with the demand for cheap and abundant labour by the colonial masters, led to the migration of a large number of labourers from the Bhojpuri region of the country to European colonies like Mauritius, Suriname, Guyana, Fiji and Trinidad. Out of them, 34,000 Bhojpuris migrated to Suriname, at that time a Dutch colony between 26 February 1873 and 24 May 1916. They were recruited as indentured labourers to work on the Surinamese plantations of sugarcane, coffee, cotton, cacao and so on. Some generations later, around the year of Surinamese independence in 1975, a large number of Surinamese Hindustanis migrated to the Netherlands. With more than 100,000 people today, these Dutchmen of Hindustani descent constitute a significant minority group within Dutch society. In Suriname, the Hindustani population that was left behind numbers some 150,000 people. The Surinamese Hindustanis, the Dutch Hindustanis and the Bhojpuris of India share a common cultural heritage as an outcome of their common point of origin in India. That this common culture has withstood the test of time can be evidenced from the fact that even after so many generations one can observe a striking similarity in the oral culture of these three sets of people.

The colonial migration that took place from the Bhojpuri region of India wrought a major upheaval in the entire area. The impact of this phenomenon was too severe to be borne either by the people who left for foreign shores or for the ones who were left behind. It was a heavy emotional loss for almost every family that was difficult to be gauged or understood. Before they realized, many tender relationships were torn apart: wives from their husbands, sisters from their brothers, a father's old-age support who was an apple of his mother's eye. As can be evidenced from the narratives of the family members who were left behind, the migrants just seemed to vanish into thin air. Few of the people left behind knew that their loved ones were leaving for far-off foreign shores from where they might never return.

The pain and suffering that emanated from this emotional loss resulted in a folklore and cultural tradition in the form of songs, dances, theatres and other cultural productions. These cultural performances and folk traditions were coping mechanisms to bear with the loss of the loved ones. Many rituals, customs, prayers and beliefs also emerged in these regions that were usually performed by women to ensure the long life and well-being of the near and dear ones who had departed for far-off places. As in the colonial period, migration is still a harsh reality that is being faced by the people of these villages. Poverty, illiteracy, landlessness and lack of job opportunities to absorb the surplus population of these regions are the major causes of the large-scale migration that is taking from this region to places like Calcutta, Mumbai, Surat, Punjab and Delhi. The only difference is that today the migrants and their family members are well aware of the places where they are going and the length of time that they will be away and are in constant touch with each other over telephone. The nature of contemporary migration differs greatly from the colonial migration because of the change in circumstances post-independence, and migration is also far more widespread today. If we analyse the migration situation now, we will find that the idea of distance and time has also been reduced in the virtual sense due to advancement in technology and availability of quicker modes of travel.

This difference can be understood while talking to the old people of the villages who were present when overseas migration was taking place and colonial recruiters lured the people of the village away. The pain, anguish and suffering of the family members who are left behind, however, are still the same and are still being expressed in the same form as in the colonial migration. Most of these cultural forms have been handed down over generations through oral tradition although new cultural forms are constantly being created with the changing needs of the people. According to Stuart Hall, 'Cultures are forever in transition. Yesterday's rebellious subculture is today's commercial pap and today's pap can become the basis for tomorrow's culture of resistance' (Duncombe: 185). Hall rightly pointed out the problem of cultural theorists who define popular culture in two quite unacceptable poles: pure autonomy or total encapsulation. A group of cultural analysts believes culture as an autonomous whole and

CONCLUSION

the other group believes in the thesis of cultural incorporation. I observed during my analysis of popular culture of migration that this form of culture is forever in transition, it evolves, multiple additions and deletions are made to it, reminiscing and forgetting occurs in it but it always has a constitutive base, which may have trace in their root culture. In spite of hybridity, the base constituent of any culture remains intact. This base culture reflects the original culture. Culture travels, but the memory that goes along with the migrant's cultural baggage is changeable although the resonance of the root in the culture of the destination and the influence of the destination in the culture of the homeland are clearly visible. When the culture of the homeland is reframed through the influence of destination, it gets internalized in the destination and the difference of the self and the other vanishes in the homeland. However, the case may be different in the destination where multiple identities exist together and the people living there may have a sense of insecurity towards the migrants due to a fear of dilution of their own culture. Thus in order to retain their culture in an unknown land, migrants create their own visibility by celebrating their important festivals like *Chatt Puja* with great pomp and show. These festivals provide them an identity that would otherwise get lost in an alien culture.

These cultural expressions are still being used as mechanisms to cope with the present-day migration of the loved ones. At the destination points, the huge population of migrants from Uttar Pradesh and Bihar are now gradually transforming into a potential vote bank for different political parties who try to woo them to vote for their parties by allurements of better living conditions like water, electricity and housing. The cultural heritage of the migrants, especially the folk songs, with their underlying theme of migration and separation, is used to pull the crowds at the rallies organized by the political parties. At the homelands too, where migration from almost all households is a lived reality, folk songs with the theme of migration are used to get people to vote for different political parties.

In Chapter 1, 'Who migrated and why: the *bidesia* story', we described the journey of the migrants from the subdepots to Suriname. In Chapter 2, '*Bidesia* and settlement histories in Suriname', we described the various phases in the settlement history of the Bhojpuri migrants in Suriname. Chapter 3, 'Double migration and silenced history: Hindustanis from Suriname to the Netherlands', was an emotional history of the exile and separation of the Bhojpuri migrants from India to Suriname and then to the Netherlands that gave rise to the *bidesia bhav* (emotionality). Chapter 4, '*Bidesia* folk culture in the triangle: Bhojpuri region of India, Suriname and the Netherlands', gave an overview of the *Bidesia* folk culture. Chapter 5, 'Still they are migrating: contemporary migration from Bhojpuri region', described the mass migration that is still going on from the Bhojpuri region to various parts of India, especially to big cities like Delhi, Mumbai, Surat and Bangalore. Chapter 6, 'Migration and cultural productions: documenting history of cultural practices', was a documentation of the cultural productions generated in the Bhojpuri region due to migration that were produced in the colonial period and are still present there. Chapter 7, 'Migrants and politics', described how migrants are being used by various political parties in the destination points to win votes as they constitute a large vote bank and how cultural productions based on migration and separation are used to emotionally win them over. Cultural productions based on the themes of migration and separation are also used by political leaders in the Bhojpuri region to win the votes of the people there as migration is a burning issue there, with almost every family having some members who have migrated, and people are emotionally touched by this theme.

It is hoped that this book on the Bhojpuri migration, which occurred during the colonial period and is still taking place today, leaving a deep imprint in the lives of people in so many countries and whose effects are still being felt even after so many years, has been able to bring out the pathos and sufferings experienced both by the people who were uprooted from their homes and hearths and by the people who experienced the pain of seeing their loved ones go away to distant lands to face an indefinite future. This pain and suffering is still being experienced by the migrants of this region who are migrating in the present period to places like Delhi, Mumbai, Calcutta and Surat. The oral tradition and cultural heritage that emerged in the colonial period as an outcome of the heavy emotional loss and were handed down over generations are still being used as mechanisms to cope with the pain and suffering that the present-day migrants and their family members experience. For the migrants who went overseas too, these oral folk traditions were an important component of their cultural baggage, which helped them to recover from the pain caused by the separation of their loved ones in their homeland. These were carefully preserved and handed down over generations and is still flourishing among the present-day Bhojpuris living in Suriname and Holland. A study and comparison of these cultural traditions in the homeland country, namely India, and in the destination countries, namely Suriname and Holland, will be an important step in unearthing the roots of the present-day non-resident Bhojpuris and for establishing their common cultural heritage. The study was an exploration into the process of migration both in the colonial period and in the contemporary period and the emotional loss caused to the various sets of people involved in this process. Through this study, we hope to sensitize people about the circumstances that compel people to migrate and the heavy emotional price that they and their family members have to pay to earn money. As is obvious from the autobiographical narratives included in the report, no amount of money is large enough to compensate for the emotional loss and suffering experienced by the migrants at their destination points and their family members in their homelands. Thus through this study, we would like to develop intervention strategies to sensitize people about the pain involved in this process so that further outflow of migrants from their homelands can be reduced and people can be motivated to improve conditions in their native places.

# BIBLIOGRAPHY

Adhin, J. H. (1998 [1957]). "Eenheid in Verscheidenheid" in L. Lichtveld (ed.), *Culturele Activiteit in Suriname: Beginselen, Feiten en Problemen*. Paramaribo: Stichting Cultureel Centrum Suriname. pp. 134–139.
Bahadur, G. (2013). *Coolie Woman: The Odyssey of Indenture*. Gurgaon: Hachette India.
Bajnath, K. (1979). Een overzicht van de Sarnami literatuur (scriptie Leiden 1979). p. 19.
Bhagwanbali, R. (2010). De Awatar van Slavernij: Hindoestaanse migranten onder het indentured labour system naar Suriname 1873-1916. Den Haag: Amrit.
Birbalsingh, F. (ed.) (1993). *Indo-Caribbean Resistance*. Toronto: Ontario Society for Studies in Indo-Caribbean Culture.
Brereton, Bridget, and Winston Dookeran (eds.). (1982). *East Indians in the Caribbean: Colonialism and the Struggle for Identity*. New York: Kraus International.
Carter, Marina, and Khal Torabully. (2002). *Coolitude: An Anthology of the Indian Labour Diaspora*. London: Anthem Press.
Chakrabarty, D. (2002). "Memories of Displacement: The Poetry and Prejudice of Dwelling" in *Habitations of Modernity: Essays in the Wake of Subaltern Studies*. Delhi: Permanent Black. pp. 115–137.
Choenni, C. and Choenni, C. (2012). *Sarnami Hindostani 1920–1960. Worteling, identiteit en gemeenschapsvorming in Suriname (Rooting, identity and community building in Suriname)*. Amsterdam: KIT Publishers.
Damsteegt, T. (2002). "Sarnami as an Immigrant koiné" in E. Carlin and J. Arends (eds.), *Atlas of the Language of Suriname*. Leiden: KILTV Press. pp. 249–263.
Damsteegt, Theo. (1990). "Hindi and Sarnami as Literary Languages of the East Indian Surinamese" in Mariola Offredi (ed.), *Language versus Dialect: Linguistic and Literary Essays on Hindi, Tamil and Sarnami*. Delhi: Manohar. pp. 47–63.
De Klerk, C.J.M. (1953). *De Immigratie der Hindostanen in Suriname (The Immigration of Hindustanis)*. Amsterdam: Urbi et Orbi.
Deva, I. (1989). *Folk Culture and Peasant Society in India*. Jaipur: Rawat Publications.
Duncombe, S. (2002). *Cultural Resistance Reader*. London: Verso.
Dwivedi, B.P. (2000). *Bhikhari Thakur: Bhojpuri Ke Bhartendu*. Allahabad: Aashu Prakashan.

Erickson, Edgar L. (1934). "The Introduction of East Indian Coolies into the British West Indies" in *The Journal of Modern History*, 6, 2.

Gajadin, C. (2005). A Silenced History: Hindustani Migration to Suriname and Holland, Bidesia Project- Country Report The Netherlands. KIT: Royal Tropical Institute.

Gautam, M.K. (1995). "Challenge and Change: The Indian Diaspora in Its Historical and Contemporary Contexts." *Paper presented in the Conference on the Indian Diaspora*, Trinidad, University of West Indies, St. Augustine, 11–18 August.

Gooptar, P. (2014). *The Impact of Indian Movies on East Indian Identity in Trinidad*. Lambert Academic Publishing.

Grierson, George A. (1883). *Report on Colonial Emigration from the Bengal Presidency*. Calcutta.

Grierson, George A. (1886). "Some Bhojpuri Songs" in *Journal of Royal Asiatic Society*, Part-18, pp. 45.

Hassankhan, Maurits S. (2013). "Kahe gaile bides – Why Did You Go Overseas? An Introduction in Emotional Aspects of Migration History: A Diaspora Perspective" in Kumar Mahabir (ed.), *Caribbean Issues in the Indian Diaspora*. Delhi: Serial Publications. pp. 3–35.

Hassankhan, Maurits S. (2014). "The Indian Indentured Experience in Suriname: A Discussion of Control, Accommodation and Resistance" in Maurits Hassankhan, Brij Lal and Doug Munro (eds.), *Resistance and Indian Indenture Experience: Comparative Perspectives*. Delhi: Manohar Publications. pp. 199–240.

Hill, Arthur Harvey. (1919). "Emigration from India" in *Timehri*, 6.

Hoefte, R. (1998). In Place of Slavery: A Social History of British Indian and Javanese Laborers in Suriname. USA: University Press of Florida.

Kadri, Hifjullah, M. and Hassan N. Kadri (eds.) *Barahmasa Neh*. Rampur: Rampur Raja Library.

Kamlesh, K. (1992). "Pravasi Hindi Lokgeeton Men Vedana Ke swar" in *Manav* (Lucknow), 22, 1, pp. 1–7.

Khan, Munshi Rahman. (2005). *Jeevan Prakash: The Autobiography of an Indian Indentured Labourer*. Delhi: Shipra Publications.

Kishna, S. (1983). "Het ontstaan van het Sarnami" in E. Charry, G. Koefoed, P. Muysken, and S. Kishna (eds.), *De talen van Suriname*. Muiderberg: Coutinho. pp. 67–92.

Klerk, C.J.M. de (1953). *De immigratie der Hindostanen (The Immigration of Hindustanis)*. Amsterdam: Urbi et Orbi.

Kolff, Dirk H.A. (1990). *Naukar, Rajput and Sepoy*. Cambridge: Cambridge University Press.

Lal, Brij V. (1980). "Approaches to the Study of Indian Indenture Emigration with Special References to Fiji" in *Journal of Pacific History*, 15, 1, pp. 52–70, London: Leicester University Press.

Majumder, M. (ed.). (2010). *Kahe Gaile Bides: Why Did You Go Overseas?* Allahabad: Mango Books.

Mangru, B. (1993). "Tadjah in British Guiana" in F. Birbalsingh (ed.), *Indo-Caribbean Resistance*. Toronto: Ontario Society for Studies in Indo-Caribbean Culture. pp. 13–26.

Manuel, Peter (2000). *East Indian Music in the West Indies: Tan-Singing, Chutney, and the Making of Indo-Caribbean Culture.* Philadelphia: Temple University Press.
Marhé, R.M. (1985). *Sarnami Byákaran: Een elementaire grammatica van het Sarnami.* Leidschendam: Stichting voor Surinamers.
McNeill, James, and Chimman Lal. (1915). *Report on the Condition of Indian Immigrants in the Dutch Colonies: Trinidad, British Guiana or Demerara, Jamaica and Fiji and in the Dutch Colony of Surinam or Dutch Guiana.* British Parliamentary Papers, the British Library.
McNeill, James and Chimman Lal. (1915). *Report on the Condition of Indian Immigrants in Four British Colonies and Suriname.* Edinburgh: Her Majesty's Stationary Office.
Mohapatra, Prabhu P. (2004). *The Politics of Representation in the Indian Labour Diaspora: West Indies, 1880–1920.* Noida: V.V. Giri National Labour Institute.
Naidu, Vijay. (1980). *The Violence of Indenture in Fiji.* Suva, Fiji: World University Service, in association with the University of the South Pacific.
Narayan, B. (2005). *Bidesia: Migration, Change and Folk Culture.* Allahabad: NCZCC.
Prakash, J. (ed.) (2006). *Autobiography of an Indian Indentured Labourer: Munshi Rahman Khan 1874–1972.* Translated by Kathinka Kerkhoff. New Delhi: Shipra Publication.
Raghoebier, Pt. R. (1987). *Sanskriti ki baten. Bijdragen tot de kennis van de Hindostaanse Cultuur in Suriname.* Paramaribo: Ministerie van Onderwijs, Cultuur en Wetenschappen afdeling Cultuurstudies.
Raman, A. (1984). *Phulon ke Panchi (Bird of Flowers).* Paramaribo: Sanatan Dharm Mahasabha.
Ramsoedh, Hans and Lucie Bloemberg (1995). *The Institutionalization of Hinduism in Suriname and Guyana.* Paramaribo: Leo Victor (Surinaamse Verkenningen).
Richmond, Theophilus. (2010). In David Dabydeen and Ian McDonald (eds.), *The First Crossing: Journal of Theophilus Richmond.* Georgetown: The Caribbean Press for the Government of Guyana.
Rosenwein, B.H. (June 2002). "Worrying about Emotions in History," in *The American Historical Review*, 107, 3, pp. 821–845.
Singh, D.P. (2001). *Bhojpuri Ke Kavi aur Kavya.* Patna: Bihar Rashtra Bhasha Parishad
Singh, K. (1991). *Poorvanchal Ke Shram Lokgeet.* Allahabad: Parimal Prakashan.
Singh, Rajkumari. (1998). "I Am a Coolie" in Ian McDonald (ed.), *They Came in Ships: An Anthology of Indo-Guyanese Prose and Poetry.* Leeds: Peepal Tree Press.
Speckmann, J.D. (1965). *Marriage and Kinship among the Indians in Surinam.* Assen: Van Gorcum.
Srivastava, S. (1937). *Prayag Pradeep.* Allahabad: Hindustani Academy.
Tiwari, B. Narayan (2002). *Bidesia: A Study of Folklore and Migration, an Explorative Documentation.* Jhusi, Allahabad: G.B. Pant Social Science Institute.
Tiwari, B. Narayan, Nivedita Singh, Prakash Narayan Tripathi and Mousumi Majumder. (2005). *Bidesia: National Indian Report.* Allahabad: G.B. Pant Social Science Institute.
Tiwari, R.N. (ed.). (2013). *Bhojpuri Shrama Lokgeeton mein Jantsaar.* Kolkata: Pratishruti Prakashan.
Tinker, Hugh. (1993). *A New System of Slavery.* London: Hansib Publishing.

Totaram, Sanadhya. (1991). *My Twenty-One Years in the Fiji Islands*. Suva, Fiji: The Fiji Museum.
Upadhyaya, K. (1999). *Bhojpuri Lok geet*. Prayag: Hindi Sahitya Sammellan.
Van Kempen, M. (1987). *De Surinaamse Literatuur. 1970–1985: Een Documentatie. Paramaribo: De Volksboekwinkel*. [Bibliography of primary and secondary sources of Surinamese literature, with a comprehensive introduction].
Van Kempen, M. (2003). *Een geschiedenis van de Surinaamse Literatuur. Band I & II Vanaf de orale literatuur tot het jaar 2000*. Breda: De Geus. [History of Surinamese Literature. Vols. I & II From the Oral Literature up to the Year 2000].
Vatuk, Ved Prakash. (1964). "Protest Songs of British Guiana" in *The Journal of American Folklore*, 77, 305.
Walter, R. (1981). *A History of the Guyanese Working People: 1881–1905*. London: Heinemann Educational Books.
Yadav, M. (2014). *Birha Darshan: Itihaas, Sanskriti aur Parampara*. Delhi: Manak Publications.
Yadav, Veerendra Narayan and Nagendra Prasad Singh (eds.). (2005). *Bhikhari Thakur Rachnavali*. Patna: Bihar Rashtra Bhasha Parishad.

# INDEX

agriculture 109, 134, 144–5, 154–5, 159
Allahabad 4, 20, 31–2, 41, 89, 107, 109, 125, 129, 135, 153
arkatiyas 21, 26–8, 39, 74, 79, 108
*Arya Samaj* 52
aspirations 54, 102, 105, 135–6
audience 17, 76–7, 97, 100, 158
autobiographical narratives 17–19
AVROS *(Algemene Vereniging Radio Omroep Suriname)* 53

Baderi village 4–5
Bahri, Hardev 134
*baithak-gana* 24, 49, 54, 57, 82–8; in Netherlands 86–8; recent trends in 88
ballad 9, 135–6
barahmasa songs 13, 75, 140–4
Barwaripur village 11, 112, 116, 119, 151
base culture 4, 161
Bhabha, Homi K. 4
*bhaiya* 21, 24, 107
Bhojpuri cinema 156
Bhojpuri community 9
Bhojpuri culture 111, 137
Bhojpuri films 96–7, 153
Bhojpuri folk consciousness 12, 73–4
Bhojpuri folk culture 8–10, 65, 96, 157–8
Bhojpuri folklore 69
Bhojpuri folk songs 10, 68–9, 138, 140, 144; popular 158
Bhojpuri Indians 2–3, 60
Bhojpuri language 96–7, 158
Bhojpuri migrants 17, 20–1, 23, 38–9, 77, 137, 156–7, 161; first-generation 3

Bhojpuri region: contemporary migration from 20–2
Bhojpuris 1–4, 9–10, 14, 17, 21–2, 24, 40, 42, 59, 78, 85, 95–7, 100, 156, 159
*bidesia* 10, 65, 67; in ship 33–6
*bidesia bhav* 10, 13, 15, 17, 19–20, 23, 161
*bidesia* folk culture 2, 10, 21, 23–4, 93, 161; in India 64–74
*bidesia* folklore 77
*bidesia* folk songs 13, 66, 74, 77; composition of 10, 65
*bidesia* folk theatre 75–6; tradition 12–13
*bidesia* folk tradition 10, 65–7, 77
*bidesia nautanki* 74–7
*bidesia* theatres 13, 74–6
*bidesia* villages 111
Bihar 1, 17, 20, 23, 40–1, 62, 95–6, 107–9, 111, 134, 137–8, 153, 157, 161
Bihari, Rameschander 88
*biraha* songs 70, 82, 133–6
Bombay 30, 38–9, 53, 62
Brahmins 32, 39, 46, 154
British Caribbean 1, 47
Burley, J. 34

Caribbean countries 1, 7, 40, 42, 45, 65, 79, 89, 93, 95, 97, 134
Chaitoe, Ramdew 86–8
Choenni, Gharietje 100, 102
chutney songs 85, 87
colonial migration 147, 159–60
communities, emotional 5, 9–10
contemporary migration 20–2; from Bhojpuri region 107–31

169

coolie depot 29
cooly schools 47
cultural baggage 2–3, 36, 49, 82, 161–2
Cultural Centre of Suriname 90
cultural heritage 2, 5, 19, 42, 60, 82, 86, 97, 161–2
cultural practices 133–52
cultural productions 18, 22, 24, 93, 160, 162
cultural representations 133, 147
culture 2–4, 8, 19–22, 24, 40, 42–4, 46, 49, 53–4, 62, 83–4, 88–9, 95–7, 133, 160–1; migrant 4; peasant 40; popular 9, 21, 111, 160–1; unique Indo-Surinamese 44

*Daak Main* 150–1
*daffadars* 28–9
deserted wife 114–15, 131
destination points 5, 8–9, 13, 17, 21–2, 24, 77–8, 95, 108–9, 134, 151, 154, 156, 158, 161–3
destinations 2–10, 13, 15, 17–19, 21, 23, 35–6, 48, 71, 107, 112, 118, 131, 147, 161
diaspora, second wave of 54–7
diasporic community 5
double migration 59–63
Dowson, William Frank 26
dramas 2, 10, 50–1, 64, 89–90, 94–5
*Dui Lumber* 38
Dutch Hindustanis 3, 24, 60, 62, 100, 159
Dwijram, Sri Ram Sakal Pathak 66, 74

East Indians 7–8, 46–7, 52–3
*Ekhtiar aur Hak* 48
emigrants 6, 32, 92
emigration agents 26–7
emigration office 16–17
emotional community 5–12
emotional pain 15–16
emotions 2, 6–10, 16–17, 22, 100, 139–40, 147, 156

families, immigrant 69
farmers 5, 32, 35, 103, 109–10
farm labourers 109–10

fear psychosis syndrome 69
Fijian folk song 13
folk culture 2, 9–10, 21–4, 65, 82, 93, 96, 111, 133–5
folklore 2
foreign shores 1, 64–5, 159–60

Gajadin, Chitra 100
Gautam, Brijendra 112, 116, 135, 137, 154, 157
genres, popular Bhojpuri folk song 137, 139
Gokhale, G.K. 7

Hall, Stuart 160
Hassankhan, Maurits 45
Hindustani community 41–2, 49, 54, 63, 88, 90, 95
Hindustani culture 53, 86
Hindustani folk drama 91–3
Hindustani immigrants 44, 62, 92
Hindustani migrants 47
Hindustani music 82–6
Hindustanis 2–3, 40–3, 46–52, 54–7, 59–63, 79, 82–4, 86–94, 97–100, 161
Hindustani Surinamese 24, 62, 86, 93, 97; language of 24, 97–9
Hindustani women 61
homeland India 53
households 6, 41–2, 111, 117, 120, 128, 130, 155–6, 161
hybridity 4–5, 161

immigrants 18–20, 27, 32–6, 42–9, 52, 57, 79, 81, 98
immigration 44, 92
Immigration Ordinance of British Guiana (1893) 19
indenture 6, 15–17, 22, 49, 51
indentured migrants 7, 15, 19, 36
indentured migration 6–7, 9, 11, 13
indentured subjectivity 19–20
indentureship 8, 23, 44–8, 50–1, 93
India: *bidesia* folk culture in 23, 64; languages in 9, 97
Indian Bhojpuri culture 4
Indian culture 52, 56, 61–2, 86, 88; export 90

# INDEX

Indian diaspora 6–7, 88
Indianization 61–3
Indian immigrants 44, 48, 84;
  trajectories 8
Indian labourers 6, 26–7
Indian languages 56, 89
Indo-Caribbean Culture 50
Indo-Caribbean diasporic Indians 40, 42, 44
Indo-Surinamese drama 24, 88–90
Indo-Surinamese immigrants 45

*jantsar* songs 144–7
Jaunpur district, village in 153, 155–6
Javanese immigrants 44
*Jeevan Prakash (Life's Light)* 18

*kahe gaile bides* 10, 24
*kajari* songs 72, 140
*kala pani* 12, 34, 71–4
Kanpur 27–30, 32, 39, 119, 129
Kempen, Van 89–90
Khan, Munshi Rahman 18, 27, 32–4
Klerk, De 40

labour contractors 21, 107–9, 126
labour songs 147
Lal, Brij V. 6
language, prestige 56, 96–8, 100

Mahabharata 52–3, 83, 91, 135–6
Majhauwa 107, 111–12, 122–3, 127, 129
marriage 19, 49, 66–7, 112, 121–3, 139
*Matla Jahaj* 38
Mauritius Bhojpuri folk song 15
men: narratives of 125–31
migrant Bhojpuris 2, 10
migrant folklore 156–8
migrant labourers 2, 10, 73
migration 4–12, 30; contemporary 20, 107, 111, 160–1; and politics 153–8
Mirzapur 29–30, 41, 125–6, 140, 153

*nautanki* (musical theatre) 2
Netherlands 1, 3, 23–4, 45, 53–4, 56–7, 59–64, 86–8, 92–4, 97–101, 159, 161; *baithak-gana* in 86–8; Sarnami

language in 99–105; settlement in 59–60
Niranjan, Goeroepersad 93–5
non-resident Bhojpuris 2

plantation life 17–19
poems 17, 21–2, 79, 97, 99–100, 102, 105, 133, 136, 140–1
political parties 24, 52, 54, 154–7, 161–2
*poorbi* songs 137–8
post-indentureship 48–9
Punjab 20, 107, 109, 127, 160

Raman, Amarsingh 79
Ramayana 2, 82–3, 91, 135–6, 138
Ramdas, Raj 100, 101
Ramkhelawan, Krish 88
recruiters 21, 23, 26, 28–9, 80, 108–9

Sanderson Commission 6, 7
Sankata Mata 147–9
Sarju, Ambika 38–9
Saraswati, Dayanand 52
sardars 18, 28, 32, 35
Sarju, Baba Ambika 29
Sarnami language 4, 24, 40, 42, 49, 54, 56, 62, 89–91, 95, 97–102; Bhojpuri and 95–7; in Netherlands 99–105
Semra village 125
separation, narratives of 111–12
separation, sense of 17–19
Sharan, Shri Nath 66
Singh, Kishor Mahtab 79
Stearns, Carol 6
Stearns, Peter 6
subdepots 23, 27–8, 29, 32, 36, 161
*Sundari Vilap* (Dwijram) 66, 74
*Surinaamse Immigranten Vereniging* 48
Suriname: *bidesia* folk culture in 77–86; diaspora, second wave of 54–7; Hindustani music in 82–6; independence and 54–7; modernization and 52–4; (re-)construction and 49–52; and settlement 38–44
Surinamers, third-generation Hindustani 99
Surinamese Hindustanis 3, 24, 62; large number of 3, 57, 159

171

Surinamese languages 56
Surinamese plantations 45, 159
Surinamese society 49, 93

Thakur, Bhikhari 12–13, 38, 65, 67, 74–7, 84, 107

Trinidad (1899) 19
Tripathi, Ramnaresh 30

women 8, 12–13, 16, 61, 64, 68–9, 75, 91, 119–20, 125, 141–2, 151; migrants 23; narratives of 112–25
World War II 49, 52, 90

For Product Safety Concerns and Information please contact our EU representative GPSR@taylorandfrancis.com
Taylor & Francis Verlag GmbH, Kaufingerstraße 24, 80331 München, Germany

www.ingramcontent.com/pod-product-compliance
Lightning Source LLC
Chambersburg PA
CBHW061835300426
44115CB00013B/2398